Debbie Evans
87-88

THE FUTURE IS NOT WHAT IT USED TO BE

Also by Warren Johnson

Muddling Toward Frugality

THE FUTURE IS NOT WHAT IT USED TO BE

RETURNING TO TRADITIONAL VALUES IN AN AGE OF SCARCITY

WARREN JOHNSON

DODD, MEAD & COMPANY New York

To Covelo

Published by Dodd, Mead & Company, Inc.
79 Madison Avenue, New York, N.Y. 10016
Distributed in Canada by
McClelland and Stewart Limited, Toronto
Manufactured in the United States of America
Designed by Trish Parcell
First Edition

Library of Congress Cataloging in Publication Data

Johnson, Warren A.
The future is not what it used to be.

1. United States—Social conditions—1980–
2. United States—Moral conditions. 3. Economic
development—Environmental aspects. 4. Social values.
5. Self-interest. 6. Quality of life—United States.
I. Title.
HN59.2.J63 1985 306'.0973 84-10338
ISBN 0-396-08396-X

Contents

PREFACE: THE FINER CHALLENGE

The power and the wealth created by modern society overwhelmed traditional ways. Whatever one's attitudes toward the new or the old, affluence made debate almost irrelevant; affluence was the proof of the superiority of the new.

Yet few will disagree that something was lost in the process, and it could well be the losses that we end up feeling the most acutely. If affluence is inexorably eroded by higher prices for resources, capital shortages, budget deficits, and declines in world trade, we will experience the darker side of modern ways—the unemployment, the feeling of powerlessness, of being trapped in a monolithic economic system without the old supports of extended family, community, comforting beliefs, and roots in a familiar place.

As we slowly come to realize that our economic problems are not a temporary setback but are part of a long-term deterioration in the once favorable conditions of industrial society, people will begin to search for more satisfying ways to live than by the values of the marketplace—of strident individualism, competitiveness, accumulation, and personal autonomy. Under conditions of scarcity, these values will turn into a source of conflict and personal isolation, of fighting more tenaciously for the ever smaller amount of wealth and power available, rather than a source of progress and individual achievement as they did under conditions of abundance.

Scarcity is, after all, the more universal condition of human existence, and because of this the universal values are ones such as loyalty, generosity, and cooperation. As we move toward scarcity, we too will learn to appreciate these values once again, as values that make it easier to live with scarcity, and live well. The genius of the best ways of the past is that they permitted much to be done with little. Lives lived on a simpler, less material plane were made rich and full. This will be our challenge, too, as we move toward scarcity.

If this seems like a difficult challenge, it should be remembered that we have much to work with even if our worst fears about depleting oil fields, unemployment, and economic deterioration materialized. We have an abundance of land and all the renewable resources that go with land; we have the tools and the scientific understanding to use them; we have time to change; and most valuable of all, we have an incredibly rich cultural heritage to draw upon. To cling to a declining way of life would be to deny our own past. Our ancestors chartered a new continent. We will be charting a new way of life, one that can be sustained long after the last coal seam has been emptied. Ours is the finer challenge.

1
The Value of Restraint

Although we pride ourselves on our ability to look at things rationally, we seem not to notice a basic contradiction in the way we see our world and the directions in which we are moving.

On the one hand, there is a widespread feeling that we have made a great deal of progress in expanding individual freedoms and removing barriers that interfered with the full development of the individual. What remains to be done, from this perspective, is to complete this process, to shed the last of the ignorance and the repressions of the past so that individuals can take the last steps to what is a fully modern consciousness, one which is able to utilize the extraordinary advances of the modern age. At the same time, there is a very different but equally common feeling that there has been a major deterioration in the quality of life in this country, that there has been a loss of many cherished ways, of much that is beautiful and healthful, and that just getting by is growing increasingly difficult and unpleasant, even dangerous.

We can have these two seemingly contradictory trends at the same time because they are one and the same phenomenon. The long-standing movement toward greater individual freedom has worked out to be a reduced willingness to restrain oneself for the benefit of others. Private gains have too often been at the expense of the general well-being.

It wasn't meant to work out this way, of course. Each freedom was also to entail a responsibility, and the expectation was that we would exercise our freedom in constructive ways. But under the impact of a series of historical forces, this did not happen. The lack of restraints favored those willing to exploit the opportunities that were appearing. The benefits of a new machine or a rich ore deposit went to those who were most aggressive in taking advantage of them. The free enterprise system virtually required that each of us look out for ourselves; no one else would. Our political process required that we push for our own interests; everyone else was, and if we didn't do the same thing, we would miss out.

All restraints, in fact, when seen from the position of one person, can be seen as barriers, as something that stands in the way of one's freedom to take advantage of a situation. It is only from the perspective of the community, however defined, that restraints have value, where the net benefit can be positive, a benefit to all. With our thrust toward individualism, however, these restraints had very little support and have fallen away steadily, until today there is a very large sphere of behavior in which anything is permitted.

That individuals have all manner of problems in our society is not disputed; the figures for alcoholism, drug addiction, mental illness, crime, divorce, and suicide all suggest that there are many people who, for many different reasons, are suffering rather than thriving on the extraordinary advances of these times. But shouldn't there also be people who are able to utilize the advances effectively? Yet how often do we come into contact with individuals who have achieved a full, balanced life, doing creative, fulfilling work but not driven by it, who are surrounded by close friends in a human environment of trust and who have the time and the ease of mind to enjoy the abundance our society provides? There are no formal barriers to this, as far as I can see, yet such success does not seem to be common. What we do have thrust in front of us as success, more often than not, is the example of a person who has exploited the real opportunities our society provides, who has been single-minded enough to push to the top, doing whatever is necessary to get there and gain "honor, power, riches, fame, and the love of women," in Freud's phrase. Who can say that this is not a natural result of a large-scale society built around a maximum of individual freedom and a minimum of restraint?

The possibility that such a way of life may not bring happiness rarely crossed our minds; its logic seems so straightforward. Nor did we put much credence in the selfless actions that the ways of the past regularly called for. Indeed, it only proved their idiocy, for certainly, if something is important to us we must go out and get it; that seems obvious. To restrain the freedom to get what we want and replace it with obligations toward others, came to be seen as contrived by the old order who would benefit from it. We found all sorts of reasons for rejecting these obligations—for justifying our self-centeredness.

Yet it remains disturbing that our self-seeking behavior rarely brought the satisfactions we expected, especially compared to selfless action. Why does it feel so good, for example, to be able to help other people? Why should the spoiled child be so unhappy compared to the child who carries a full share of the family tasks? There is something here that is missed in our rational assessment of where the good life is, something that lies deep in the human psyche. *The theme of selflessness appears time and time again in the wisdom of the past, and it is a source of happiness, satisfaction, and fulfillment rather than the oppression we make of it. Selflessness, the subjective theme of this book, could make restraints functional in terms of personal human satisfaction as well as public well-being.*

Ironically, when talking about the bad times of the past, the most common example that comes up is the factory system of the early industrial era in which owners did not hesitate to work people twelve and fourteen hours a day and to put children in the workshops too. If we have made progress, it is most unambiguously demonstrated in the *restraints* placed on these early excesses of the free market system, a system which saw all interference in the free market as bad. One freedom—free trade—was given primacy over all others, the tyranny of the marketplace.

Balance

All this is not to say that the answer is authoritarian political or economic systems. Far from it; that would be going from one extreme to the other. Freedom is an extremely valuable possession, and the market is a useful device for facilitating exchange. But if one person's freedom means the exploitation of others, some form of restraint is called for, and just because the free market is a good way to organize a Saturday market does not mean it is a good basis for organizing an entire society. Many things are valuable in moderation that are undesirable in excess. The need is for balance—in this case, balance between the needs of self and society, between individual freedom and general well-being.

But beyond that, we are out of balance in many other ways, in the size of our institutions and our cities, and in our utilization of technology. There is a need to balance our short-term economic needs for raw materials with the needs of our descendants, and to find the balance between conserving values from the past and encouraging creativity and change. Above all, we need a balanced view of human nature, as having the potential for good as well as for bad. To restrain the bad is less pleasant than to encourage the good, but without such restraint the good may well be lost as no longer functional in a world increasingly shaped by those willing to exploit other people and nature in any way they can.

How we came to create such imbalances is a complex question, but part of it is clearly associated with technological advance in the modern era. The incredible power of our machines gave credence to the idea that we were like gods, almost a different species from other peoples whose archaic ways kept them from enjoying the fruits of progress we enjoyed. Even now, there is a common feeling that, with our modern knowledge and understanding and the experiences of recent years, new answers must be found. Answers from the past cannot possibly be of use to us; we are beyond all that. Our modern consciousness is our proudest possession, the source of our pride and, some would add, our arrogance.

There is, of course, much in the present that is good, unambiguously so—nutritious food, medical knowledge, scientific understanding, the treasures in libraries, on records and tapes, and rapid communications. But most of these stem from advances in science and technology, as opposed to an understanding of what leads to human happiness. And there are torments in the modern world too which everyone is familiar with. Our understanding of the past, in contrast, is inevitably secondhand and faulty; we cannot experience it. And what we do know often stems from the times when older ways were breaking down, when old loyalties were standing in the way of new opportunities and when old certainties were turning into anachronisms. The prudery of the Victorian era, for example, was a futile effort to deny the changes spreading through our society as it turned from an agrarian society to an industrial one.

Still, we find ourselves with contradictory feelings about the past. The forward-looking parts within us see the past as torment and toil compared to our ease and comfort, while our fears and frustrations cause us to see the past nostalgically, as somehow a golden age. Both are unrealistic. Both lack balance. Nothing is all good, just as nothing is all bad; everything has its costs. And besides, the clock cannot be turned back anyway (as we hear so often), regardless of what we may wish. And this certainly applies to going back to the conditions of the American frontier as well, with its openness and opportunity that shaped the American character so deeply. The clouding of technological advance and the end of cheap resources means that the last of the frontiers has been settled, and now we will have to live with what we have. There is not going to be a Homestead Act for space settlement or a wide-open scramble for its mineral wealth. From now on, it may well be the historians, the anthropologists, and the natural scientists that have more to offer us in shaping the future than the technologists.

To argue that the time-tested ways of the past will be valuable in the future is not to argue that the future will be like the past, far from it, but only that they are both shaped by the same force—scarcity. As abundance slips away from our grasp and the industrial economy weakens, our heritage of traditional wisdom will increasingly be seen as a storehouse of truths that have been winnowed from the long experiences of human existence, out of the always difficult task of people living together. Unless we wish to deem our ancestors irrational, their ways must have some value. *Our task is to revitalize them—to give them new life—in the situations we find ourselves in.* As with any resource, this collected wisdom should be evaluated on an ongoing basis for its usefulness, in much the same way that a mineral resource, for example, is continuously evaluated for its contribution to society. Only to ignore a resource, whether out of pride or ignorance, is to unnecessarily impoverish the future.

Ripeness

A number of traditional ways never died out completely, especially those relating to family and friends. Ties with those closest to us form a valuable center to our lives, making it easier to deal with an outside world that is often cold and threatening. Loneliness is the great curse of modern life for those without such ties. This outside world is also the one that overwhelmed communities in the past and ran roughshod over ethical systems, which were built on words that now have a vaguely antique sound to them—humility, duty, steadfastness, loyalty, charity, brotherhood, honor, and reverence. Machines and the free market system had no regard for obligations to family or community; to produce as efficiently as possible was all that mattered. There is no reason to believe the same forces are not at work now, which means that some of the more powerful traditional ways will be difficult to use, for a while at least. Community today still struggles against fragmentation, against the pull of different ideas in different directions. And religion, trying to overcome a history of intolerance and religious wars and seeing its ethical systems violated so pervasively in our society, has too often been reduced to a private matter, passive and compliant, or has spent its energies raging against a few modern transgressions when a whole way of life is involved. Both religion and community introduce discordant notes into the otherwise clear signals our society gives us, signals characterized by the words we hear so often—power, freedom, control, individual rights, free choice, property rights, and self-fulfillment. The political process reflects the demands of constituent groups which try to direct the costs or benefits of government actions one way or another, to management or labor, the wealthy or the poor, the majority or minorities, the taxpayers or tax beneficiaries. Rarely do questions of responsibility, fairness, or obligation enter, on either side of the political spectrum.

But times change, and attitudes change with them. We supported our economic system enthusiastically as long as it produced more and more goods and greater opportunities, but as the economy slips toward stagnation and decline we will see the darker side of this system—the unemployment, the feelings of powerlessness and isolation, of being trapped in a monolithic system with little capacity to change it, and without the old supports of extended family, community, and comforting beliefs. As it sets in that this is not a temporary downturn but part of a long-term deterioration in the once favorable conditions of industrial society, people will begin to search for more satisfactory ways to live their lives. We already see renewed interest in community and religion, the linchpins of traditional society. Changes occur when the times are ready, when conditions move to a point where they make such good sense that they cannot be stopped, changes that, if tried prematurely, could not have been made to work. Cultural evolution is a slow process. Great leaps forward are not characteristic of it, as China found to its loss during the cultural revolution. Cataclysmic changes, when they do occur, are apt to be destructive. A smooth, steady evolution is the most that can be hoped for, of people adapting to conditions as they emerge, not prematurely but not resisting change either.

Cataclysm?

But cataclysmic change is possible. It could occur in any number of ways in a world that has become so interdependent: nuclear war, disruption of international trade, worldwide depression, or a breakdown in law and order. It is such issues that Robert Heilbroner dealt with in *An Inquiry Into the Human Prospect*. Cataclysm cannot be dealt with in the same way as something such as the slow depletion of natural resources. No one knows what the likelihood of collapse is, and steps taken to avoid it may be a waste if it does not occur. Nor is it possible to know which one might occur, when, or where. Planning for nuclear war, for example, would mean doing something different than planning for social breakdown. And given the interdependencies in our society, it may be impossible to avoid the consequences of any catastrophe, regardless of which one occurs. Fear, up to a point, can be useful; it motivates people to take action and to work for a better future. But obsessive fear can lead to wasted efforts or even become a debilitating force if it discourages any action at all.

The only way to deal with unknowns of this magnitude is to assume that they will not happen—that mankind will survive—and for each of us to search for positive steps to take. There is at least an element of self-fulfilling prophecy here, for if we act as if we expect the worst to happen, whether nuclear war or economic breakdown, it is much more apt to happen. Rather than seeing the future as something we have no control over, it should be seen as evolving out of our actions today, out of a large number of small decisions that each of us make every day. If we continue to push, for example, for higher wages, lower taxes, and increased military power, and then expect politicians to pull off the miracles necessary to make all this work, then perhaps we ought to prepare for the worst. But if we do this, then we should realize that collapse is the result of our own decisions, of our unwillingness to accept the world as it is, rather than something OPEC or the Russians have done to us.

Even for those who despair about the prospects for collapse or nuclear war, the only useful response is action. To be without hope is to be defeated, and ultimately this is a crime against the human spirit and against our children. We have no choice but to take courage in our hands and plunge into the tasks ahead of us, and to make the best of what we have to work with. Work is a healing force, a way to find out what we are capable of, to learn that we can live on less and work with others once again. It is up to each of us to begin building for a sounder way of life, not only for ourselves but for our children too.

In other words, radical steps or political organization are not necessary or even appropriate at this stage. The process of cultural evolution stems from modest changes in our ideas of what is important, and moving in those directions whenever possible. As competition grows more intense for fewer economic rewards, for example, the age-old functions of family and the community become more apparent, as cooperative institutions that permit people to pool resources, to work together in a secure social environment, and to enjoy things that would be beyond the reach of a single individual. If the national political process grows less responsive to our needs, the tendency will be to shift away from dependence on its decisions and to move toward a greater reliance on those closer to one's life. In such situations, status will be determined by how much an individual contributes to the general well-being of a community rather than by how much he can take from it in private wealth. It is such a community that can be expected to pull together rather than to grow more divisive if times get tough. Economic behavior will change in many ways as well. Rather than the risks of investing, economic goals will gravitate toward the older ones of preserving a valued and secure way of life, the best gift parents can hand down to their children. There will be a turning away from a preoccupation with continually higher material standards and individual autonomy, and a turning toward a more sustainable way of life within a richer human community. To the degree we succeed in this, the dangers of nuclear war and economic or political collapse will decline.

The Sustainable Economy

These changes will proceed slowly. They can be seen, in part, as an effort to avoid being too dependent on the industrial economy and its problems, which are beyond the control of any individual. Still, the stage on which the initial actions will be played out will be the economy; it is the major organizing force in our society today, and also the first part to change in response to scarcity.

In all likelihood, we can look forward to the evolution of a dual economy. One part is the *industrial economy*, which we are all familiar with. The other one is increasingly being referred to as the *sustainable economy*; Lester Brown of The

Worldwatch Institute explored its implications in *Building A Sustainable Society*. It is called this not so much because it is indeed sustainable but because it is a conscious movement in that direction, a movement toward the use of renewable resources whenever possible and away from the industrial resources which we are consuming so rapidly. The sustainable economy is the opposite pole from the economy foreseen by Herman Kahn in *The Coming Boom*, and is even substantially different from the economy suggested by John Naisbitt in *Megatrends*, which looks toward technological advance to sustain modern society in the face of scarcity. We are certain to try to do this since it is what Americans are counting on to avoid more fundamental change. The sustainable economy, however, assumes that technological advance will not be adequate to sustain the world as we know it, and that the future will inevitably require more use of human muscles, simpler tools and machines, less transportation, and a simpler material standard of living, but with compensations in terms of a way of life that is on a more human scale, richer in cooperation and community, and less dependent on a fragile and declining industrial economy.

The sustainable economy will advance in parallel with the decline of the industrial economy, but both economies are essential and there is no reason to assume there will be conflict between them. We are all dependent on the industrial economy today, whether we want to admit it or not, not only for most of our day-to-day needs but also for the tools and the materials necessary to build the sustainable economy. The sustainable economy is equally important, not only because it is where the alternatives appropriate to the era of scarcity are being developed, but also because it will act as an outlet for the pressures generated within the industrial economy, especially unemployment. The sustainable economy will increasingly be the only alternative as jobs are lost, as is happening in a number of industries today. And anyone who voluntarily gives up a job in the industrial economy will make it a little bit easier for those who stay, leaving a job for those who have no taste for the sustainable economy. The amount of unemployment will be a measure of how smoothly—or roughly—the transformation of our society is taking place.

The Individual

Because this is such an individualistic age, let us begin with the individual. Anything else would be futile. Even so, right from the start it will be assumed that one of the objectives of individual action will be to avoid the loneliness and the insecurity of our times and to reestablish ties with others to share the burdens and the joys of the coming times when so many changes are to be expected. No reasons will be offered for inaction because of bad government, big corporations, or any of the other common excuses for doing nothing. The only motivation for change will be the individual decision that each step is in one's own long-term interests, the result of a rational assessment of where the good life is. If individual prerogatives are given up, it will only be to obtain something of greater worth.

The next three chapters speak mostly about the deterioration of a way of life that we have grown accustomed to, about such things as unemployment, falling purchasing power, and debt, subjects that are mundane at best, depressing at worst, especially when not much is said about what will take its place. Readers who find this subject uncongenial, can skip ahead to Chapter 5, where the questions become more cultural—more human—and less mired in the dismal science of economics. Readers who had read *Muddling Toward Frugal-*

ity can do this and miss very little; only the emphasis here is somewhat different; it is more on the options individuals have to move toward the sustainable economy and less about economic policy. These chapters are included because it is the barriers facing industrial society that are causing individuals to change today. If the sustainable economy is to provide a sound basis for an enduring way of life, it must be based on a realistic understanding of where we are now and what our economic choices are. That is the first task.

2
The End of an Era, Not the End of the World

Scarcity may have unsettling implications for industrial society, but these are no different from the implications that industrialization had for other peoples. Millions of people have been caught up in the maelstrom of change in recent centuries, changes which we, who benefitted from them, rarely think about. The best example in this country is the gradual impoverishment of millions of small farmers, if only because we have better statistics for farmers than for the untold numbers of small shopkeepers, craftsmen, miners, and lumbermen, who also saw their livelihoods destroyed by forces beyond their control. The experiences of farmers tell us quite a bit about the process of economic change in our society, a process that is certain to continue. And it is something that we would be well served to be familiar with because it is not pleasant to be on the wrong side of economic trends that are destroying one's livelihood.

An Era Ends

The farm population in the United States fell from 30.5 million people in 1940 to 7.9 million in 1977, its lowest point, a drop of 74 percent in thirty-seven years. This process left farming areas with a feeling of old age, abandonment, and decay that has been hard to overcome. Houses and stores were boarded up since there were often no buyers at any price. Rural areas became backwaters, perhaps with a few big farms and metal sheds full of machines, but few workers, not enough to keep the community alive, its schools and churches open, or the sound of children on the sidewalks. The young people were the first to leave, looking for jobs elsewhere, and the community that was left was increasingly characterized by old people, poor old people, and abandoned homes and barns. In 1960, 18 percent of all farm families had incomes below $1,000! This was the era when the farm population was falling the fastest, and the very low incomes are a measure of the economic pressure being exerted on farm families to get out of farming and head for the cities. In the end, most farmers had no choice.

To get a feeling for the scale of this change in the farming community, imagine that employment in the auto industry fell at the same rate for thirty-seven years, decimating at the same time other industries—steel, rubber, glass, and plastics—that supply the auto industry. Imagine the population of cities such as Detroit falling at the same rate, from 4.4 million to 1.1 million. Think of all the abandoned dwellings, the bankruptcies, the lost businesses, of all the heartbreak of people caught up in economic forces beyond their control. All they could do was watch as everything they worked for came to nothing.

This is what happened to the majority of farmers. They

tried to resist the forces that were working against them, and the government tried to help too in a number of ways, but it didn't work. The economic trends were too strong. Bigness was essential to survive, and there was no way for all the small farmers to become big. It was a hard time, but the change was made. There was no revolution or economic collapse.

The free market is a very effective device for forcing such changes (putting aside the question of whether the changes were good or bad). Cold, impersonal market forces drive uncompetitive enterprises out of business, a job that would be very hard to do any other way. If large industries are undermined in the future as the farmers were in the past, or if unemployment drives people from cities, should we be surprised? Could we not, just as easily, say "What's new? This is the American way." The fact that most farmers did not want to leave the way of life they knew and head for the cities with their intimidating ways did not make any difference. That's just the way things were. That's our free enterprise system.

Farmers found themselves in a very common trap during this period when technological advance was so rapid. They could see how much work the new farm machines could do, but they also saw how expensive they were. The only way to utilize these machines profitably was to use them on large acreages, but few farmers could afford to buy not only the new machines but more land as well. Most small farmers had two choices, two ways to go broke. They could go broke quickly buying the machines but not being able to use them on enough land to earn the money to make their payments. Or they could go broke slowly without buying the machines and trying to live on a declining income as the new machines brought down the cost of growing food—and the prices the farmers received for their crops. The larger farmers could make a living at these prices, but they meant poverty for small farmers. In 1960, the *average* annual farm income was $2,907, which includes the incomes of the larger farmers too! We now look with nostalgia on the 1950s and 1960s as good times, but farmers did not see it that way; their low incomes are what caused houses and barns to remain unpainted and junk to accumulate. Farm poverty subsidized cheap food in the cities, contributing to the good life there.

The trends were there, but because they were so disturbing there was a tendency for farmers to deny them. They assumed that if they just worked harder they could overcome the disadvantages they temporarily faced and get back on a good footing. The hope that kept farmers going was that the prices of the crops they sold would someday go back up so they could live a bit easier. Farming was, after all, known to be the most secure way of life. Land was the true source of wealth in the traditional way of thinking, and few farmers wanted to be known as the ones who were beaten and leave a community where their roots had been for generations and move to the cities, which they often distrusted. But the fossil fuels were too powerful and too cheap, and without industrializing a farmer could not compete.

As farm machines grew larger and more efficient, life for small farmers grew harder. Rather than seeing their crop prices rise, the farmers saw the new machines drive them down further, and debts piled up against the farm. When the end finally came, many families had no capital left to get started elsewhere. If they had been able to see these changes coming, they could have sold out and headed for the cities earlier, avoiding the toil, the poverty, and the crushing of the spirit brought on by this inexorable process. And there was no reason why they couldn't have changed earlier, but it was a hard thing to do, to give up a familiar way of life for one in the cities that was unknown and, to most of them, unattractive.

A Modern Sequel?

Could we write the same story for industrial America, as the beginning of the steady erosion of a once prosperous way of life? The ominous trends are certainly there. Markets for many products are glutted, which means that prices are weak and some producers are being forced out of business. Foreign competition is becoming stiffer, especially from east Asian countries, and governments are responding to political pressure to preserve jobs by erecting trade barriers or subsidizing their own industries, both of which threaten the international trade on which most nations of the world now depend. Third World countries are buying fewer manufactured goods because they cannot borrow the money to pay for them, and the debts they have already accumulated threaten many large banks, and indeed, even the world monetary system on which trade depends. Robots, computers, and automation improve a country's competitive position, but reduce the need for labor. Unemployed workers not only spend less money but they also weaken the ability of other workers to get pay raises, both of which tend to reduce the money consumers have to purchase goods, accentuating the problem of glutted markets.

In order to stimulate flagging demand, supply side economists persuaded Congress to pass tax cuts that gave a temporary boost to the economy, but the cost was high —huge federal deficits. They may have pushed America toward the kind of situation enveloping the Latin American economy, where the money supply must be increased faster and faster to avoid an increasingly severe recession or depression.

There are positive signs as well. The American economy has been very creative in developing new products and services, and the economy has shown great resiliancy in coping with the stresses of recent years. But still, the stresses are growing. The Japanese and other foreign countries are making inroads into other industries, prices could weaken further, and more jobs could be lost as demand weakens. Tax revenues could drop and accumulated debts could constrict our ability to deal with the problems we face. Even now, the list of industries on thin ice is fairly long—airlines, banking, farming, building, steel, autos, trucking, mining, logging, and the energy companies that over-invested during the energy boom. Add to this the government programs in Social Security and Medicare that are unlikely to be able to meet the obligations they are accumulating.

There is one key difference, of course, between the decline of the agrarian economy in the past and the decline of the industrial economy that has just begun—there will not be the other booming sectors of the economy for displaced workers to turn to as there were for farmers. But everything else is much the same. Housing prices are weak because there are many homes on the market but few buyers. Retail sales lag as industry payrolls decline, so merchants are hurting and salespeople are laid off. Local and state tax revenues fall, public services are reduced, and demand for unemployment assistance increases. Maintenance begins to suffer, and young people leave, looking for jobs elsewhere. The outlines of the trap are clearly discernible. It is a precarious place to be. A society that is organized around the market can become a tough place to be when the economic forces turn against an industry, a city, or a region. But just as with farmers, it is tempting to sit tight and hope things work out. This is especially true today because the major alternative, the sustainable economy, is unattractive to people who are used to a regular forty-hour-a-week job with a good income. It is much easier to assume that things will get better with a new administration, new economic policies, or new technology; "something" will happen to keep things going. But as it looks today, the slowdown will not be temporary. Raw materials are the lifeblood of the industrial economy, and the blood is getting thin.

Raw Materials and the Industrial Economy

There is a very human tendency for people to assume that there is an answer to our economic problems, one that will preserve our way of life as we know it today. But going against this hope is one absolutely fundamental factor—the increase in raw material prices relative to labor. Higher prices are the surest indicator of scarcity, reflecting the increased capital and effort needed to obtain raw materials from lower quality or depleting resources. Higher prices for raw materials tell us in the clearest possible way that the era of rising incomes and economic growth is over.

The prices of raw materials fell for centuries as machines took over work that was previously done by men and beasts in the mines, forests, and farmlands. This trend continued all through the boom years of the postwar period as machines grew larger and more efficient. But in the early seventies, raw material prices bottomed out and then shot up as increasing standards of living worldwide finally caused the demand for raw materials to outrun the supply. Between 1970 and 1982, the index of *Crude Materials for Further Processing* in this country increased from 112 to 327, and most of this stemmed from higher energy costs, which increased almost *ninefold* on the wholesale level. The oil industry is strong, but miners, loggers, and farmers are still hurting because their costs are high while demand for their products is weak, leading to low prices. *Energy has clearly emerged as the limiting factor in the industrial economy.*

There are two reasons for higher energy prices, and they are not greedy oil companies or bumbling politicians. One, of course, is OPEC, which was able to capitalize on energy shortages in the industrialized countries to jack up its prices. But they couldn't have done this so successfully if it hadn't been for the second reason, the high cost of the domestic alternatives we have, whether offshore oil and gas, synthetic fuels from coal and oil shale, nuclear energy, or renewable resources such as solar and wind. *OPEC oil is still a good bargain compared to our own sources, which is why we import so much of it.*

Americans tend to assume that higher energy prices should be covered by cost-of-living increases, but unfortunately, higher energy prices mean just the reverse—that incomes should fall since more of our national wealth must go into obtaining it. Rather than getting all the oil we need from our older, low-cost oil fields in Texas and Louisiana, as we could in the past, American workers must now produce goods for export to pay for imported oil, goods that we used to be able to consume ourselves. And think of the billions of dollars that must now be spent every year exploring for new oil deposits, developing arctic or offshore fields, building pipelines, and the billions more that would be needed to develop synthetic fuels from coal or oil shales. This money has to come from somewhere, and the only place to get it is out of the consumer sector of the economy—out of our paychecks. But this was unacceptable to Americans accustomed to continually rising living standards. Instead of accepting scarcity and living with the higher costs, we asked for and usually received cost-of-living increases, so we could go on consuming as if scarcity did not exist. But scarcity cannot be denied so easily, and the higher incomes only created stagflation—both inflation and unemployment—inflation because higher incomes allowed us to live beyond our means and unemployment because labor remained expensive compared to machines.

This process is described more fully in *Muddling Toward Frugality,* which I wrote in 1977. The trends noted there have largely continued: energy prices doubled again, the economy continued to weaken, and incomes began to fall behind inflation. But incomes did not fall as much as the higher cost of raw materials would have suggested, and in hindsight the factor that I did not foresee then was the willingness of the nation to go into debt to sustain its affluent ways. The $200 billion federal deficit for the 1983–84 fiscal year is an infusion into the American economy of *$850 per person!* Think of how deflationary a balanced budget would have been on the economy that year. Private and corporate debts too have exploded, especially since the second oil shock of 1979–80. In 1982, the worst year to date, 45 percent of the profits of American business went to servicing their debts. Farm debt now is 12 times farm income, and in 1983 almost half of farm income was from the government. Debt now hangs like a black cloud over many businesses, governments, and individuals, and has led to the highest bankruptcy rate since the Depression. Financial stringencies have driven down the money governments spend to maintain their roads, utilities, and buildings from 4.1 percent of GNP in 1965 to 1.7 percent in 1983. In other words, by going into debt we have managed to hold on to our high standard of living and avoid facing up to scarcity, but only at ominously high costs in terms of debt, reduced maintenance of our physical plant, as well as unemployment and inflation. Trying to deny scarcity is a risky business; it cannot be done, not for long at least.

Energy is the backbone of the industrial economy. It is what does our work for us, moving our cars, running our machines, bringing water to farm fields and cities, moving the products of industry to markets, as well as being embodied in all the products of the petrochemical industries, the synthetic fabrics, the plastics, and the fertilizers that make our agriculture so productive. Without energy, our lives would be much more like life in the past or in underdeveloped countries today. Energy makes all the difference. It makes us modern.

Ninety percent of the energy we use today comes from the fossil fuels—oil, natural gas, and coal. They are nonrenewable; once used they are gone. Oil and gas are the premium fuels because they are so concentrated and easy to use. Think of what 1 gallon of gasoline can do, pushing a car, say, 20 miles along a mountain road, and then imagine trying to push that car the same distance by hand! If we could drink gasoline, we could live on the calories in 1 gallon for twelve days! It is powerful, concentrated stuff, far superior in every way to coal, the fossil fuel we have in abundance. But our reserves of oil especially have been declining steadily; between 1970 and 1980, our proved reserves fell from 39 billion barrels to 29. With our consumption at roughly 6 billion barrels a year, our reserves would last us only five years if we had to rely on them alone. Average annual discoveries during the last five years have been 1.8 billion barrels a year, less than a third of our consumption, even with high rates of drilling in response to high oil prices. H. William Menard, former director of the

U.S. Geological Survey, stated in an article in the January 1981 issue of *Scientific American* that recent drilling experience has confirmed earlier estimates that the end of the century will see domestic oil production down significantly, as much as two-thirds in the lower forty-eight states. Alaska remains the last great hope, but there have been no major discoveries there since Prudhoe Bay in 1968. These are items that rarely make the newspapers; they are too disturbing.

The optimists point out that the proved reserves of oil elsewhere in the world are some twenty times greater than our reserves, that OPEC needs us as buyers as much as we need them as sellers, and that we can export food to pay for the imported oil we need. This *may* be true, but it still leaves us with an unsatisfactory dependence on the Middle East and its unstable politics and proximity to the Soviet Union. We do have huge deposits of coal and oil shales, which is fortunate, but these fuels are messy to mine and use, and the cost of turning them into synthetic oil and gas is so huge that even Exxon gave up on them when the recession depressed oil prices.

Because of the cyclic nature of the economy there is a tendency for public attitudes to flip-flop on the issue of energy, from unnecessary pessimism when gas lines form to unjustified optimism when oil prices drop a bit. Reality probably lies somewhere in between, along the line of average prices rather than the extremes. Scarcity is most likely to come slowly over a number of decades as the better resources worldwide are used up. And prices, while trending generally upward, will also reflect the state of the economy. Strong economic growth would inevitably put upward pressure on oil prices, while a severe recession would see prices fall, perhaps significantly. *But the prospects for both steady economic growth and lower energy prices are poor,* to say the least. The pattern of recent years seems likely to continue, with each recovery shorter than hoped for and each recession deeper and longer.

Because of the bleak prospects for increased energy supplies, attention is finally shifting to the efficiency with which energy is used. From the long-term perspective, this is where it should be, trying to get the most from the energy we have rather than simply trying to get it out of the ground faster. And since we used energy so wastefully in the past, we have fine opportunities to conserve today. Much progress has already been made, by driving smaller cars, insulating homes, and improving the care with which energy is used. The next steps, however, will be more expensive, and some are not feasible at all. Our cities, for example, cannot be turned from sprawling, car-oriented ones to compact cities built for walking and public transportation. And a good part of the lowered energy consumption so far is not so much a matter of improved efficiency as it is simply getting by with less, as many Americans got by without a new car in 1980–82. Consumers can undoubtedly survive without so many new cars, but it was hard on the workers in Detroit who lost their jobs. Conservation is the bright side of reduced energy use; energy is being used more efficiently. Recession is the dark side; there is less work being done. We are making progress, but it is far from painless.

Beyond all the questions of energy supplies looms the largest question of all: *How will the economy behave under conditions of raw material scarcity and declining production?* The Marxists have argued for years that capitalism cannot survive without growth, not without depression or runaway inflation anyway, and there is some disturbing support for this point of view. If falling incomes force people to reduce their consumption, this would cause further plant closings, a process that could snowball into a depression, speeded up by the heavy debts many businesses carry today. If widespread bankruptcies threaten, there would be tremendous pressure on the Federal Reserve System to stem the slide by increasing the money supply, adding the specter of runaway inflation to that of unemployment. Who can say that this process has not already begun?

It is not difficult to come up with all sorts of doomsday scenarios that contrast strikingly with the "business as usual" quality of most business reporting, in which the only questions seem to be about the recovery and how strong it will be. Again, reality will probably be somewhere in between, disappointing both the Marxists and Wall Street. Changes are occurring, but they are far from either a smooth adaption to scarcity or revolutionary change. Still, it is a perilous business, all the way around. The most conservative economic policies are the safest ones in such a situation, policies that encourage jobs, even if lower paid, the sharing of available work, and the reduced use of energy. All of these are complementary—using labor to save energy—but they are not the sort of things that excite voters or, therefore, politicians. For some time yet, we will probably continue to ask politicians to do the impossible, to bring back the open, growing economy of the sixties, and politicians, being only human, will continue to fall over each other trying to convince voters they can do it.

It is important to keep in mind that the spokesmen for the economy will generally present optimistic information about how it is doing because this helps to sustain it, helps to keep people buying products and making investments. This is important, since it is people's expectations that largely hold the economy together, that keep people from taking their money out of the banks or bailing out of the stock market, triggering a classic panic that would not do anybody much good. Expectations of "business as usual," however, could do a great disservice as well if they discouraged necessary adjustments to a changing situation. Government and business in this regard have a symbiotic relationship; both are dependent on a strong economy, business for profits and government for tax revenues. It is not surprising then, that there is little enthusiasm for information that undermines confidence in the economy.

Individuals, however, have everything to gain by realistic expectations of what is ahead, at least as realistic as it is possible to be in these changing times.

False Solutions

In such unsatisfying circumstances it is not surprising that a number of false solutions have received wide currency, solutions that make people feel better about what they are doing and thus sustain the world as they know it. We feel there must be an answer.

Reindustrialization. Using computers, robots, and automated equipment to increase productivity is one of the most common and generally accepted ideas for overcoming the effects not only of costly imported oil but of foreign competition as well. The logic seems solid enough, at first glance anyway. With the new technology, American workers will be able to produce more. They will produce not only the goods and services we are accustomed to having ourselves but also the goods we need to export to pay for imported oil. Higher productivity would mean we could buy the oil we need and enjoy a higher standard of living as well.

But there are several problems associated with this otherwise happy solution. First, reindustrialization requires a great deal of capital, and the only true source of this capital is savings. But savings are low in this country compared to other industrial nations, and the government takes much of what is saved to cover its debts. If the government bribes people to save with tax advantages, the cost gets high in terms of lost tax revenues, increasing the size of the federal debt. Saving means giving up consumption today in order to have more in the future, something we seem reluctant to do.

Second, American exports must compete for markets with efficient European and Asian producers, something that is becoming more difficult as world markets become glutted. Glutted markets mean depressed prices and suspicions that foreign countries are dumping steel, textiles, shoes, and other products to keep their own workers on the job. And the debt problems of less developed countries are forcing them to cut back on their purchases of imported goods.

But most fundamental of all is the fact that increased productivity would entail *less use of labor* and *more use of machines, energy, and materials.* Less labor would be needed to produce a product; that is the definition of higher productivity. This would be no problem if there were a continuous need for improved machines, since this would provide steady jobs making the new machines and manning them. This was the way things were in the past when productivity gains were steady and the economy was growing. That sounds fine. The trouble is that it runs head-on into our basic problem, the limiting factor of energy. Steadily increasing energy supplies would be needed to sustain this steady growth, whereas the reality we face is declining energy supplies and higher prices. *Increased production cannot be the answer to scarcity.*

This is where the problem of continued high wages becomes

so important. Robots and computers are purchased by businesses because using these machines is cheaper than using labor. Robots and computers are, in reality, job killers rather than job producers. Already their production is going overseas, where costs are lower. Reindustrialization, under today's conditions, may make sense in terms of international competition, but in a basic sense it is all wrong in that it uses additional energy to displace labor. But this is happening largely because wages have remained as high as they are here. The resistance to falling wages means, in effect, that unemployment will remain high, American products will be less competitive, and we will continue to invest in ways to increase productivity when we should be investing to increase *energy productivity*—to obtain more work out of the energy we have—and to use labor to do this.

Yet higher labor productivity remains the focus. Why is this? Partly it is because of the need to compete with foreign producers, but much more than that, higher productivity is the process that raised our standard of living in the past, and this comfortable idea dies hard. Improving energy productivity, in contrast, does nothing for our material standard of living. It just means we drive smaller cars and spend money to cut down high energy bills in homes, factories, and office buildings. Americans much prefer to conquer problems, rather than just learn how to live with them. But if we did manage to get the capital needed to improve labor productivity, all we would succeed in doing would be to push energy prices higher and create further unemployment, perhaps to produce goods for which world markets are glutted, and consume scarce capital to do so. We would be using capital in ways that look to the past rather than to the future and the limiting factor of industrial society—energy.

The ideal investment would be one that increased both

labor and energy productivity, and this is quite often possible. The steel industry provides a good example. American steel is being undersold by Japanese steel, which is produced more efficiently in modern plants in terms of both labor and energy used. We have been unable to match Japanese labor productivity even in our most modern plants, but gains can be made with new mills, and energy productivity could also be improved by 20 to 30 percent. It sounds like a good investment. But the cost of a new steel mill is high, $3 to $4 billion, which means that the savings would have to be large enough to offset the interest costs of capital used to build it. Adding further to the risk is the worldwide surplus of steelmaking capacity as many countries try to be self-sufficient in this basic material. On top of that, steel consumption has fallen, partly because cars grew smaller and fewer were sold, suggesting that the squeeze on the steel industry is here to stay. In 1982, plant utilization was 43 percent of capacity. Such low demand for steel would make it very difficult for a steel company to cover the cost of new mill construction, threatening it with bankruptcy. Yet not spending the money would mean a continuing loss of the steel market to the Japanese.

This turns out to be the same problem farmers faced in the past, that of being unable to afford the newest machines but unable to compete without them. What to do? One answer is to restrict foreign imports, but that only risks retaliation, something that is dangerous for a country that is so dependent on exports for jobs and to pay for imported oil. Federal financial assistance to build new plants wouldn't change what is basically a poor investment, only shift the costs—and the risks—to the taxpayer. That doesn't help. The only answer is the one the farmers were forced to—lower wages. It is the high pay of steelworkers, more than anything else, that makes American steel more expensive than foreign steel. But how much less satisfying this is than in the past, when there were no barriers to the use of any new machines we could build, improving incomes in the process.

In fact, our labor productivity has been declining for several years, and although the reasons for this are complex, energy has much to do with it. We now must do much more work to obtain each new barrel of oil than before. Coal, because it is a solid, requires more work in handling than oil and gas, which slip conveniently through pipelines. Railroads and waterborne transportation both use less energy than trucks, but require more labor in handling materials since trucks can go from door to door. With less energy available to the economy, the obvious alternative is to use more labor to save energy, but this is, by definition, lower productivity. Without a dramatic breakthrough in energy, our productivity will continue to decline, and the dreams of reindustrialization will disappear under the impact of unemployment, capital shortages, and bankruptcies caused by the wrong investments.

The Electronic Revolution. Electronic devices are quite attractive since they use energy and materials so efficiently. A telephone call slips across wires with very little energy behind it, and increasingly without even a wire at all. The result is that a telephone call is still cheap and the telephone company makes handsome profits, while the price of a postage stamp goes up regularly and the post office struggles to get out of the red, primarily because mail must be physically trundled across the country, using far more energy while going much slower.

But this does not mean it is correct to project the expansion of the electronics industry straight on to what has been called the information economy. The predictions that electronics would make obsolete such things as money, libraries, newspapers, and even the trip to the office have not materialized, not to any great extent anyway. Credit cards are inconvenient to use in most cases, and the service is not cheap. The cost of putting even a modest-sized library into a computer is more than can be justified. The distribution of newspapers and magazines by electronic media, which would be so advantageous to publishers faced with high paper and postage costs, is still too costly to be done. To work at home, even with all the communications technology to bring the work there, still does not bring one's colleagues or customers there, and dealing with these people is often the most important part of a job. It is often the most enjoyable too. We are social animals, and sitting at home in front of a video screen does nothing for our social instincts.

Much has been made of the miniaturization of calculators, computers, and other electronic devices, suggesting that this process can be extended widely throughout industrial society, thus reducing raw material and energy demands greatly. But the food we eat or the clothes we wear cannot be miniaturized, and if cars and houses are miniaturized, it will not be because we want them that way but because that is all we can afford. No trend line can be projected straight ahead without looking at what kind of country it passes through.

The same is true of the service economy, which has been expanding for a number of years as manufacturing jobs have gone overseas. But to assume that the service economy can expand indefinitely is not justified either. Already, a good part of the millions of unemployed Americans are from the "smokestack" industries that are no longer competitive, and the service industries have not been able to absorb them. And think how much more difficult our economic situation would be without the production of farmers, for example, who are able to export 60 percent of their wheat crop to help pay for imported oil. And the profits of one of our largest service industries—banking—are tenuous indeed given the financial situation of many of the nations they have loaned money to. No, we have to earn our way in the world just like any other nation. We are not guaranteed a favored status simply because we had a head start over other nations in the industrial era.

Increased Oil and Gas Production. Because our economy was built for cheap oil and gas, another widely accepted solution is to go all out to produce more of these fuels from our own resources. This makes sense in the short run since, to the degree it is successful, it reduces imports and makes the things we have built useful again. But it does so only by using the energy that would otherwise be available later on. There is oil in the ground yet to be discovered, and given enough incentives, it will be found. But for what purpose? To keep the freeways jammed and the air polluted? If we sustain consumption now, it will be at the expense of the future, at the expense of our children who will be left with the well-nigh impossible task of building a low-energy society very rapidly but without the high-grade oil or gas needed for the task. And if we leave them heavily in debt, it will be a mean-spirited legacy indeed.

The policy of all-out production now should actually be called the "drain America fast" policy. It is analogous to another shortsighted policy of the past, the "drain America first" policy of the fifties and sixties when restrictions were placed on the importation of then cheap Arab oil in order to protect domestic producers in Texas and Louisiana. How we would like to have that domestic oil still in the ground now!

The farsighted policy today would be to *extend* the life of the oil and gas we have left by placing a tax on it to discourage use, and by so doing give a financial incentive for conservation and the use of common fuels such as coal and solar energy, which would not be taxed. But taxes are not popular; we are looking for easier solutions, preferably ones that someone else pays for. All-out production comes closest to it.

Deregulation. In our frustration in trying to deal with what may well be an insoluble problem, it becomes very easy to find scapegoats, and the government is a common target.

Is it the fault of excessive governmental regulations that our economy is stagnating? Partly so; much regulation is ineffective and costly, often designed to protect various special interest groups. But some regulation has been constructive too. If federally mandated improvements in automobile fuel consumption had not been enacted, Detroit would have been hurt much worse by the second oil shock of 1979–80 than it was. Other regulations provide us with benefits, even if inefficiently. Many were made necessary by the competitive nature of the economy. Without pollution controls, for example, a manufacturer who voluntarily invested in pollution control equipment would be rewarded for his public-spiritedness by losing out to competitors who kept their costs down by doing nothing about pollution. Regulation is the only way to make sure that everyone competes under the same rules. We may have gone too far in this direction, but regulation will always be needed. And while deregulation may make the adjustment to scarcity somewhat easier, it cannot bring back affluence.

Reduced Government Spending. Are our economic problems the result of excessive government spending? Partly so;

the government spends more money than it takes in, which leads to higher interest rates and inflation, and a good part of what it spends is wasted. But the government provides many important services as well, such as defense, education, highways, and parks, as well as social security for the elderly and protection against devastating medical expenses. Are these more or less important than what individuals would spend a tax cut on? It's a matter of opinion. In terms of new energy sources, anyway, the government is far ahead of the private sector. The government did virtually all the early research work for nuclear energy, synthetic fuels, and subsidized solar energy when consumers were reluctant to invest on their own. Industry seems very willing to let government do all the expensive high-risk pioneering work, and then take over when a profit looks likely.

If we cut taxes for middle- and upper-income people and reduce welfare benefits, would we all work harder? Perhaps, but the United States already has almost the greatest differences in wealth between rich and poor of any industrial nation —only France exceeds us in inequality—but this does not seem to do much for our economy, not as much as the greater equality seems to do for other countries. The Japanese, with the greatest equality, work the hardest. Most industrial nations have higher taxes than we do—Germany's are half again higher—and their economies do well enough. No easy answers here.

If the government has contributed to our problems, it is primarily in running such large deficits and contributing to inflation. Yet this excess spending was done in response to public demands—to stimulate the economy, to be strong militarily, and to keep taxes down. Federal deficits are, to a degree, subsidies to all of us, providing more jobs and higher after-tax incomes. The government helped us to live beyond our means, but we asked it to do this through the political process when we pushed for lower taxes or help for ailing industries and regions. But it wasn't "free" help, as it seemed at the time. Today the per capita cost of servicing the federal debt is $300 a year for every American and rising rapidly.

The one device other countries use that we do not is the value-added tax, which is a tax on consumption. It discourages consumption and thus encourages savings, the only way to avoid the tax. And saving is what the Europeans and Japanese do better than we do; savings provide them with the capital to make necessary investments. But we seem to prefer immediate consumption, and then blame the government for inflation and high interest rates. Such scapegoating is not an attractive quality. It is an attempt to blame government for our problems when in fact the problem lies in our unwillingness to accept even the modest amount of scarcity we have encountered so far.

Government As the Answer. It is ironic that in one breath we blame the government for our problems and in the next say that the government will not allow the economy to deteriorate, or, if it does, will pay us generous unemployment benefits.

Both points of view are unrealistic. Government cannot be blamed for these problems, nor can it be expected to eliminate them. Scarcity is made up of hard physical facts of life, of depleted oil fields, dry wildcat wells, high-priced foreign oil, and huge construction costs to develop domestic alternatives. This is the reality that the government cannot change.

How will we respond to this challenge? There does not seem to be much commitment to seeing the energy question as the "moral equivalent of war." If there is a commitment, it is to private interests, and this is sure to reduce the effectiveness of the political response. We will try to do the easy things, many of which only tend to delay the inevitable adjustments, to sustain a way of life that is increasingly inappropriate. On the other hand, we are a pragmatic people, and we will strive to avoid the twin pitfalls of runaway inflation and depression, the severe problems that adversely affect everyone. These problems will force us to accept reality, but it may well be a muddled, inefficient process until we cease trying to deny scarcity.

One thing seems certain—it is a great mistake to assume that the government will take care of us. The generous unemployment benefits we enjoy today are a good example. Think of the situation the government would find itself in if the economy slowed significantly. With incomes down, revenues from personal and corporate taxes would fall, and fall rapidly because of the progressive nature of the income tax and all the corporate red ink that a slowdown would cause. At the same time, high unemployment would mean increased demands for federal assistance. The government, in short, would have its own cash-flow problem, and welfare programs could not be maintained at anywhere near current levels (including the welfare programs for special interest groups and industries).

An Era Begins

The options available to the government are everywhere restricted, which is a measure of the barriers industrial society is coming up against. But this is not the case with individuals. We have all sorts of flexibility and, unlike the process of political decision making, we can make a decision quickly. We can look forward to see where events seem to be taking us and take steps to avoid a trap, to avoid losses and disruptions to our lives. We can cut down on major expenditures, look for a more secure job in a less vulnerable region, and avoid getting into debt, which restricts our freedom to change. We can decide to enjoy simple pleasures rather than tormenting ourselves trying to reach too high and do too much. We can give up our obsession with ourselves and know the pleasures of helping others and building social ties that bring more satisfaction anyway.

Or we can rant and rave that everything is going wrong, that our freedom and opportunities are being restricted and that the world is increasingly mean and stingy with its benefits. We can ignore the very real benefits that will accompany the decline in affluence, such things as a slower paced life, a decline in air and water pollution and toxic wastes as we revert to simpler technology and renewable resources. We can decry the loss of jobs in large industries without seeing the increased opportunities for individual enterprise. We can complain about the deterioration of large cities without also seeing the renaissance of many small towns and urban neighborhoods. We can argue about who is to blame if advanced technology fails without seeing the resurgence in the use of human hands and skills. We can grow bitter over the loss of affluence and ignore the far greater opportunities for working together for a common purpose. The opportunities ahead of us are ones that will put us back in the mainstream of human history, but we may wish to remain above everyday life as others have lived it and see ourselves as technological gods reflecting a higher evolutionary stage. Then when it doesn't work out, we can find scapegoats or turn to hate and violence.

The challenge each of us faces is to see the world as realistically as possible, both the problems and the potentials. The new era is just beginning to emerge; its outlines are still vague. But there is one thing that seems certain—the transition is bound to be awkward, especially if it has to be done quickly. For everyone, the unexamined life will increasingly be a dangerous life, one that can lead into dead ends from which there is no good way out. Each of us must make our own decisions; there is no way we can shed the responsibility for making our way. To the degree we can move away from too great a dependence on the industrial economy, we will also be doing what is best for the country by reducing the pressure on an economic system that can no longer sustain the way of life it created.

3

Work in the Sustainable Economy

A visitor from outer space would find our economy hard to understand. It would seem strange that, with our immensely productive machines, we are not working only a few days a week to produce the few things humans need to survive. Instead we struggle with problems such as unemployment and depletion of resources. Why, they would ask, are we burdening ourselves with debts to build plants to produce more efficiently things that there is hardly any need for? And why does the introduction of a better machine cause some workers to face the humiliation of unemployment while the rest keep on working as hard as ever?

These things are not easy to explain (not satisfactorily, anyway, until we can delve into our deepest beliefs, which must wait until Chapter 10, the one that deals with religion). For the time being, it is the pragmatic day-to-day workings of the economy that is our concern; we all have to live with it, in one way or another. And unemployment is the most troubling issue today, according to the polls, the thing Americans fear most, more than nuclear war and crime in the streets. To be unemployed involves much more than economic hardship; it causes feelings of failure and uselessness, of having no productive role in society, of being an outsider, a misfit. Rates of alcoholism, mental illness, divorce, and even suicide fluctuate in tandem with unemployment rates in this country. And the fear of unemployment is real because the machines are so incredibly productive; there is no way to keep all workers at their places by these machines because there is neither the demand for the goods produced nor the resources to produce them with. Yet labor cannot compete without the machines; who can imagine, for example, labor taking over the work of power looms that can weave cloth at superhuman speeds, metalworking machines that stamp out metal products effortlessly, or farm equipment that can work thousands of acres of land? The answer, however, is no longer quite as straightforward as it once was.

The Vegetable Garden: A Vignette of the Future? If the large farm machines are so incredibly productive, why should 43 percent of American families have vegetable gardens (according to a 1981 Gallup Poll, an increase of nine million families since the previous poll was taken 10 years earlier)? A backyard gardener, after all, employs techniques that peasants all over the world would be familiar with.

Gardens must have economics going for them to be so widely cultivated, even if this is not the whole reason why people plant them. Still, the economic advantages are real compared to commercially grown vegetables, and they stem primarily from the *proximity* of the garden to the house, in contrast to the distance from commercial farms in Florida and

California to the local supermarket. The home gardener needs no transportation, and there are no wholesalers, retailers, or other middlemen to add their charges. There is not even any need to drive to the store to buy the vegetables. Backyard vegetables can be harvested as needed, saving processing costs, and many vegetables produce over a long season while others can be stored for long periods. A greenhouse permits production year around (and provides household heat at the same time if the greenhouse is integrated with the house). And there are no risky investments in planting a garden as there are for commercial growers. It is through such advantages that hand labor can compete with the big farm machines which, taken on their own ground, are unbeatable.

The full meaning of a vegetable garden for the sustainable economy, however, goes well beyond economics, because certainly, the hourly wage earned in working a garden cannot be very high. But there are other benefits besides cost: exercise; the fresher, more wholesome food; the aesthetics of working with the soil and turning dry seeds and composted wastes into nourishing food and colorful flowers; the knowledge gained; the pleasures of trading surpluses with friends and neighbors, or perhaps selling them at a farmers market; and the feeling of being in control of at least a small part of one's life. A simple vegetable garden can, in fact, be taken as a hopeful symbol of the future, of a world with less affluence of the type reflected in the huge array of foods in a supermarket as well as more physical work, but with the compensations that make us more alive, give us greater balance between physical, social, and mental activities, and tie us more closely to the natural environment that sustains us.

And it is a hopeful way to resolve the question of unemployment too, not only by providing work but providing it in the context of a richer human fabric than in a nine-to-five job that so often dulls the spirit—yet a job that we fight for because it is the basis for one's feeling of self-worth in this society. *From the perspective of the sustainable economy, there is plenty of work to do—the huge job of building a new way of life less dependent on nonrenewable resources.* Rather than a scarcity of work, there is an abundance, and we will need all the willing hands we can get. *And the willingness to get started will come, in large measure, from the threat of unemployment. By this simple change in perspective, unemployment can be turned from a personal and social disaster into a saving force for the future.* Nothing, not even unemployment, is all bad.

Where Are the Opportunities?

The opportunities in the sustainable economy are only now beginning to appear. Because we have only just passed the peak of affluence and still have goodly amounts of resources left, the new opportunities often have an improbable quality about them, in the same way a vegetable garden hardly seems a suitable symbol of the future, certainly not compared to the magnificent farm machines we have and the well-paying jobs we prefer to think about. But this will change as jobs grow to be more of a problem, wages fall, and work in the sustainable economy emerges as the only alternative to unemployment. Who would have thought ten years ago, for example, that the firewood industry would have grown as large as it is today, producing more energy than the nuclear industry?

The emerging economic opportunities in the sustainable economy have their origin in the very heart of our economic problem—the increasing cost of machines and energy and the falling cost of labor. The opportunities, as far as they can be seen at this early stage, fall into three general areas.

First is the provision of energy, the material that is the limiting factor for industrial society. Ideally, the focus would be the renewable resources, but for the time being it is likely to be also on the abundant forms of fossil fuels we have—coal and possibly oil shales—which will keep us going while the sustainable economy evolves. The opportunities here are not as large as might be expected.

Second, there will be opportunities to provide goods and services in less expensive and less energy-intensive ways as we grow less able to afford the affluent ways. This can be seen as simply trying to preserve a way of life as close as possible to the one we know today. If these ways seem less desirable than the ways we are accustomed to, people will still use them when the affluent ways slip beyond their reach.

The third and most significant opportunities lie in the area of decentralization, not only to avoid the cost of transportation, but, more importantly, to enable people to be closer to the renewable resources of land, water, and sunlight, which will be at the heart of the sustainable economy.

Energy Production

It is a credit to the initiative still left in this country that the response to the increase in OPEC prices has been so vigorous. From the largest corporations in the nation down to a multitude of individual entrepreneurs, a vast number of alternatives are being explored. And even though the weakening of OPEC prices has halted many of these projects, it is instructive to compare the different experiences of the two renewable resources that have seen the most activity—solar energy and firewood. The differences are quite important to individuals contemplating involvement in renewable energy resources.

Solar energy has received by far the most attention in

terms of public support, research and development funds, and governmental assistance. The flat plate collector systems that are most widely used are fairly sophisticated technologies that collect solar energy quite efficiently, especially for household hot water systems but also to heat homes and swimming pools. But because of their sophistication, these systems are fairly expensive, and only rarely can they be justified economically.

Realizing this, the solar industry pressed for governmental assistance, supported by a wide array of public groups interested in reducing the use of fossil fuels. Not surprisingly, the industry managed to get the aid in the form that favors the services it has to offer. Generous tax credits are available if you hire a contractor to install a solar system, but these are greatly reduced if you build one yourself using recycled materials, even if just as much solar energy is collected. The solar industry, in other words, acted like any other special interest group. There is nothing unusual about this, but it does present a risk to anyone considering going into the solar business; if federal tax credits are removed, say during a budget squeeze, business is apt to fall off quite substantially. And while higher energy prices would make solar systems more attractive, these prices would also reduce the money people had to buy solar collectors. The photovoltaic cells are more expensive yet, and the long fall in their prices now seems to be ending. As with so many advanced technologies, we may not be able to afford them.

A surer future for solar energy lies in simpler technology. The best one seems to be passively heated and cooled solar houses. These are competitive because the collector, rather than an expensive addition to the roof of the house, is simply the house's windows, carefully placed to collect sunlight in the winter and exclude it in the summer. Rather than expensive tanks with pumps and controls to store the energy collected, in a passive solar house the heat is stored in heavy walls and floors made of concrete, adobe, stone, or earth. In the summer, the night air is allowed in to cool the walls, keeping the home cool in the day. In the winter, the sun is collected in the day and stored in the walls and floors for the night. A house needs windows and walls anyway; building them to collect and store solar energy gives them a double use, and accomplishes this with simple technology that does not require the services of engineers or computers to control it. The only difficulty is that a solar house usually must be built from scratch; it is difficult to retrofit an existing house that was built without regard to the sun, as is the case for most American homes.

Firewood, in contrast to solar energy, was initially seen as a carryover from the past. It received virtually no governmental assistance, yet already it has grown to provide a very significant amount of energy, primarily in rural areas where woods are relatively close. And the potential for further expansion is huge. In 1977, the last time a complete U.S. Forest Service survey was made, *the forests of this country grew 50 percent more wood than was cut*, and this was during a year when construction was booming and cutting was high! Rather than *depleting* our forests, we *added* 7.4 billion cubic feet of wood to them in 1977, roughly equivalent to 60 million cords of wood. And this surplus growth has been increasing for a number of years, primarily because fast growing younger trees have replaced old growth forests and farmlands have reverted to woods in many parts of the United States. Many of these forests would benefit from the management that woodcutters can provide, for example, thinning overcrowded stands and removing less valued species and diseased trees, thus leaving the remaining trees to produce better lumber.

And the best part is that *the industry is in no way dependent on government subsidies.* When an industry takes off on its own this way, it means that it is economically competitive now; the people who work in it do not have to get into politics to preserve their jobs.

The burning of coal has much the same potential for cities that firewood has for rural areas, but unlike wood, it has many problems. Coal is the least expensive way to heat a home today, by a significant margin, and our resources are huge; we have used only about five percent of our coal resources, compared to well over half of our oil, and there is no reason why the price of coal should rise at anywhere near the rate of other fuels simply because it is so common. But coal, being a solid, is dirty to burn, dangerous to mine, and hard to handle compared to oil and gas. Regulations are likely, but they are not apt to be as strict as present regulations for industrial uses of coal are simply because coal will be the cheapest way for people to keep warm in the winter. Using coal for household heating will allow the premium fuels of oil and gas to be used for transportation and manufacturing where coal cannot be used, thus saving jobs that would otherwise be lost. Increased air pollution from coal may be one of the penalties we pay for not doing more today to prepare for the times when oil and gas grow scarce.

For many forms of renewable energy, however, the picture is far from clear. Wind energy is making progress in places where wind speeds are steady and high, but again, much of this progress depends on federal tax credits and a law which requires public utilities to buy the power produced at favorable prices. Hydroelectric energy (another old form of energy but still one of the best) has potential for expansion on the smaller rivers and streams that the dam builders overlooked, and there is a scramble to buy up old hydroelectric plants and put them back into operation. But there are no sites for new

Grand Coulees or Boulder Dams left to build on. To produce alcohol from grains never had much potential; it takes as much energy to produce the alcohol as is in the alcohol produced, and is only happening now because of the tax subsidies farming interests gained trying to develop new markets for their grains. Geothermal fields that produce dry steam are excellent sources of energy, but such fields are rare, and the more common hot water resources contain dissolved solids that have so far frustrated attempts to use them effectively. The only way to use the energy in garbage now seems to be to simply burn it to produce steam, but at some stage the raw material for even this use will decline when we can no longer afford to be the throwaway society we are today. The opportunities for passive solar heating are quite significant, but they are opportunities for builders of houses rather than makers of energy.

There will be jobs in the production of oil and gas, the premium fuels we still have, but how many jobs is impossible to say in this boom and bust industry. It has been argued that OPEC will be forced to keep the price of their oil low enough to discourage other nations from producing synthetic oil from coal or oil shales, and there is a certain logic to this argument; the synthetic fuel industry was virtually killed by the drop in oil prices in 1983. Jobs in the coal and synthetic fuel industry pay well, but most resources are in inhospitable parts of the country, such as the northern Great Plains and the Great Basin. And the work would go on against a background of opposition from local people who see their way of life being swamped by outsiders. A job here may exact too high a price.

Accommodating Scarcity

As unemployment and lowering incomes take the steam out of the economy, people will find that they are unable to buy the goods and services they could in the past. We might call this the "auto industry effect"—higher costs driving buyers away—and it will spread to other industries, especially those that rely on the heavy use of energy or are luxuries that people can get by without. The list of such goods will grow as energy grows more expensive or incomes slip. There are few industries which will not feel the pressure of sagging demand.

To find the opportunities here, the place to look is behind the problems. Ask yourself this question: When people can no longer afford something in its more expensive form, what alternatives do they have? If, for example, people have to cut back on the use of cars, this will mean jobs in other forms of transportation, such as operating a jitney line, manufacturing buses, or selling bicycles or motorbikes. With transportation increasingly expensive, people will try to drive their cars less; rather than driving to the shopping center they may walk to a corner grocery store or ask a teenage son to bicycle to a neighborhood drugstore or hardware store. Even if prices are higher, savings in transportation will make it more economical to shop nearby (and it will be more pleasant and convenient, as well). People will also look for recreation and entertainment nearby, such as at an outdoor dance pavilion in the park, a neighborhood pub, or a local movie theater. They will look for inexpensive vacations, and it may be possible to arrange chartered bus trips to resorts at group rates, or open a campground-picnic area at a nearby lake.

Every time the price of a product or a service goes up, the demand for it will weaken. And every weakening in the conventional economy will provide an opening in the sustainable economy. This is painful for those involved in the weakening industry, but it is what creates the opportunities in the sustainable economy. It also illustrates why price controls on oil and gas held back economic evolution here; cheap energy kept down the costs of affluent ways of doing things, kept the shopping centers thriving while neighborhood businesses continued to fail.

One change has already begun in response to the higher cost of transportation—the movement back into the city to be closer to jobs, stores, and entertainments. This makes sense from every perspective—in terms of energy saved, dollars saved, and time saved in transportation, as well as reversing the deterioration of in-town housing. In suburban areas it is sometimes possible for this clustering to occur around certain nodes, such as industrial sites or shopping centers, but it is far more satisfactory in older sections of cities, where housing densities are higher, shops and entertainments already exist, and more jobs are concentrated. A number of cities have already experienced this process of renewal, something that billions of dollars of urban renewal funds were unable to do, programs that instead destroyed the raw materials—the houses and shops—of today's natural regeneration.

Repair work of all kinds will expand as people find themselves unable to replace old things as easily as they could in the past. Indeed, when things such as appliances were so inexpensive (because of cheap materials and machine work) it was often impractical to repair them (because of the high cost of the repair work). In the future, the tendency will be to use labor to extend the usefulness of things, and a good repairman who can keep things going, whether a car, an appliance, or a power tool, will be increasingly valued.

When an old building is rehabilitated rather than torn down, we are in effect using labor to save materials that used to be hauled away to the dump. The person who can do rehabilitation work, which requires a wide range of skills and the ability to overcome unusual problems, will be in far higher demand than the highly specialized construction workers of today, who usually do one operation with standardized materials.

Recycling may not expand quite as rapidly as expected because it uses energy—for transportation, remanufacturing, and then transportation back to where it is to be sold again. Reuse—or renewing things without melting them down and refabricating them—avoids all of these expenses and will undoubtedly be more common. The reuse of glass bottles is growing, even without a federal bottle bill, simply because beverages in returnable bottles are less expensive than in throwaway cans and bottles. Older people are the authorities on reuse; they often speak of times when virtually everything that came into their hands was saved and reused in one way or another.

All indications are that in the future we will have more time on our hands but less money. Until recently, we had plenty of money but little time, and it made sense to have others do things for us while we used our time earning a good income and spending it. In the future, when good jobs are scarcer and we have more time on our hands but less money, we will try to do everything we can ourselves.

Decentralization

Industrial Decentralization. Our machines are often so efficient that only a small part of the cost of a product is in its manufacture. Most of what we pay goes to other things that are just as important in large-scale enterprise—packaging, transportation, advertising, wholesaling, and retailing—much of which a small-scale local producer can avoid. As some of these costs, especially for transportation, grow more significant, the local producer will find his product more competitive, even if the efficiency of his production is far lower than his big corporate competitors.

In the era of cheap energy, labor was the expensive commodity; it was the limiting factor. The companies that succeeded were the ones that could keep labor costs down by using automated machines whenever possible, and could utilize national advertising to sell goods in ever larger markets. But as energy grows expensive relative to labor, such operations will become all wrong. They will be using the expensive inputs—machines, energy, and transportation—but not labor, the one item that is beginning to fall in price. This is a prescription for failure, and it will hit many of the largest corporations that were the most successful in recent years.

Economic success in the industrial era was also based heavily on a company's ability to borrow money to make large investments in plants and equipment. Success was even measured by the ability of a firm to borrow money; profitable firms could borrow huge amounts, and they have the debts to prove it. The question is, how long will they remain assets—able to produce goods that can be sold at a profit—because if this is not the case such companies could go bankrupt quickly.

It is one thing to imagine large corporations going broke since a good number are on thin ice already. But it is harder to imagine the resurgence of small industries since they have been going down for so many years. But in recent years it has been the small firms that have made the major advances into new areas such as computers and electronics, and there are always enterprising individuals who see the new opportunities and are ready to take the risks that large corporations shy away from. The problems of bureaucracy in large firms are very much the same as in large government agencies; nothing can be done without huge amounts of money and years of development. With a new firm, everyone's prospects clearly depend on becoming profitable quickly, and these are the firms that can be expected to take advantage of decentralized production.

Agriculture again provides a good example. It is very productive today, but it is also quite energy-intensive; roughly twice as much energy is used to process and distribute food as to grow it. The farmers who can avoid these heavy energy costs will be the ones who will have improving prospects. The best way to do this is to produce for a local market, selling things fresh and without using long distance transportation, very much as the truck farmers did before they lost out to producers in California and Florida. The local farmer may even be able to reduce the use of chemical fertilizers by using wastes generated in the city. Nor will it take so much capital for such a farmer to get started since he will be using more labor and less specialized machinery, making it unnecessary, for example, to spend $200,000 for an automatic tomato picker. As buyers shift to cheaper local produce, the distant farmers will find their income dropping just as costs are climbing, and for those who are heavily in debt, bankruptcy will come quickly. The result will be further opportunities for local farmers to expand. The saddest thing here is that many American cities have built on much of the best land around them, never thinking that it might be needed for food production again.

In a number of ways, smaller cities and towns that were bypassed as manufacturing grew more centralized may find their prospects improving. They are reasonable in size and often have affordable housing. They are apt to be served by railroads or waterborne transportation, the more energy-efficient kinds. They are likely to be well located for regional manufacturing, especially if they served that purpose before the rise of the national corporations, and may have old or unused industrial facilities which small firms could move into quickly at very little cost. They may even have old machinery, further reducing the capital requirements. Older, less specialized machines that can do a number of different operations may increase in value compared to the specialized automatic machines even though they are much less efficient in terms of labor productivity. But a machine that produces spray cans or plastic toys cannot be used to make small farm implements or coal burning stoves, just as a tomato picker cannot be used to pick a few acres of corn and then moved over to the carrots.

Industrial decentralization means that less energy will be used for transportation, leaving more energy that can then be used for production. This should slow the fall in our standard of living that would otherwise be caused by reduced energy supplies. It will also mean a better balance in the distribution of our population between the largest cities and the smaller ones. But population decentralization will go much farther than the decentralization of manufacturing, and it is here that the full potential of the sustainable economy will be reached.

Population Decentralization. Rural areas have the resources to use solar energy in much the same way sunlight has sustained human existence from the beginning—by growing food, fuel, fiber, and building material. Land can be thought of as a giant solar collector, fixing solar energy in the form of plant material over a very large area; industrial society has nothing to compete with land as a way of collecting solar energy. In rural areas, water is usually available under the earth, if not in nearby springs or streams, and wastes can be disposed of in the soil, returning fertility at the same time. Indigenous building materials are available in one form or another—stone, timber, or earth. When modern materials such as glass and insulation are added, passively heated solar houses can be built that reduce the amount of supplementary fuel needed to very modest amounts. The key advantage of rural areas is the *renewable* resources they have, the ones that are not controlled by OPEC or the oil companies. *What all this means, in practical terms, is that the cost of living will be lower in rural areas, and it will be easier to get by on the lower incomes characteristic of the sustainable economy.*

To date, however, the new jobs that are appearing in rural areas reflect more the lower cost of living than the use of local resources to earn a living. The firewood industry is an exception, but the resource-based industries of today, such as agriculture, grazing, lumbering, and mining are, for the most part, large commercial activities, most of which are in depressed conditions. The new jobs being found in rural areas today are primarily due to the urban-rural migration now underway. These jobs were created to accommodate the newcomers in much the same way that jobs were created in cities when people were moving there from rural areas. Now it is rural areas that offer opportunities in retailing, services, construction, and government. Rural areas offer some of the best opportunities to start a small business because it is virtually impossible for large firms to serve these small markets. There are fewer regulations in rural areas or unions to deal with, and it takes less capital to get started. A young person can more easily find work that leads to useful skills, like helping to build a house, clerking in a store, or working in the woods, than in a city. Jobs for schoolteachers or law enforcement officers will appear as population decentralization occurs, jobs that are more rewarding in a small town than in a large city. And some industries have moved their plants to rural areas to take advantage of the more stable work force and the lower wages, although this has occurred primarily near the interstate highway network.

This is not to say that everyone will move to rural areas; far from it. Even in preindustrial times, before fossil fuels were used at all, many people lived in cities, and we will undoubtedly have more energy at our disposal than they did. What it does mean is that there should be opportunities to live in whatever sized settlements people desire, as opposed to the limited choices of the last several decades when opportunities were concentrated in the largest cities.

In an idealized way of thinking, this will mean that existing cities will not be as big or as crowded as they are now. But the reality of our economic system is that as people leave, the cities will decline economically, plagued by unemployment, falling real estate prices, and inadequate tax revenues to maintain services—the same problems that plagued rural areas in the past. Cities and industrialization developed together, and it looks as if they will decline together as well. It doesn't seem as if it should have to be this way, but if anyone knows an alternative, cities in declining industrial areas would certainly like to know about it.

Rural areas have a number of advantages today, such as less crime, traffic, and pollution; lower taxes; and a stronger sense of community. A major advantage is the lower cost of housing, the result of rural depopulation for so many years. This makes it quite profitable to trade a house in a city for one in the country and bank the savings to live on. This is probably the greatest advantage of making such a change today, when it is premature in the sense that urban incomes are still higher than rural. The rural renaissance we are seeing stems, in large measure, from the wealth that people take from cities when they move to the country.

At some stage, however, this easy transition will become

more difficult—when urban property values fall behind rural values. Then it will be expensive to move away from a city. Rural property values have been rising faster than urban values for a number of years now; the advantages of prematurity do not last forever. Even if it is not feasible to move to a rural area immediately, buying property there would still be an excellent investment, the best way to "buy into" renewable resources. It is hard to imagine how the value of rural property could not rise relative to the value of urban property unless there was some radical breakthrough on an energy source for urban industrial society.

When rural areas are no longer receiving an infusion of capital from urban areas, they will then have to face their own economic challenge—to develop their own economic base. They have the resources to do this—the advantageous renewable ones—but it will still take initiative to develop them, the same kind of innovative efforts that will be needed in urban areas to build sustainable elements into the economy.

The Prospects

It would be foolish to deny that scarcity does not have ominous implications for jobs in the industrial economy. This may be reflected in the skepticism readers feel about the jobs described in this chapter as replacing the industrial jobs lost; there is no question that they will demand more of us in terms of creativity and hard work and pay less than the jobs most of us have become accustomed to. Unemployment will be especially hard for those who have made money quickly and easily in the past or who never had to work for a few dollars an hour doing hard physical labor to get by. But by the same token, work in the industrial economy was often unsatisfying, not because it was physically taxing—we had machines for most of that kind of work—but because it was dull and repetitive, or stressful because of office politics and interpersonal rivalries. The demands of large, highly integrated business or governmental enterprises did not permit us to discover what our personal resources were, what we were really capable of.

The sustainable economy will permit this, indeed require it. The challenges we face will force us to be more alive, more resourceful. We will increasingly have to find our own opportunities, rather than have them presented to us by an employer, and to make them work with our own ingenuity and persistence. The opportunities provided will include many valuable ones: doing a broad range of tasks rather than a few specialized ones; using tools appropriate to human hands and skills rather than a remote engineering office; completing a project, rather than doing part of it repetitively; and doing work that contributes to a community's well-being, rather than disappearing into the huge consumer society where it hardly seems to matter how well the work was done. The opportunities that are emerging in the sustainable economy are ones that many people have tried for in the past, but the economic forces ran against them. Now they are running in the same direction, and running more quickly all the time.

4
Living on Less

This is the subject that often leaves people flat. At best, it seems mundane. At worst, it is downright disagreeable, with no positive attributes other than necessity.

How completely we associate the good life with what we are able to buy is a measure of our times, of how much we have been influenced by the consumer society. Consumption is seen as an end in itself, as something to be maximized, rather than a means to the good life, something to be met as easily as possible in order to leave time and energy for more important things. The pleasures of traditional life rarely involved much consumption, but were simple things such as sitting with friends over a pot of tea or bottle of wine, watching children at their games, enjoying family gatherings or holiday celebrations, walking through a busy town or out into the quiet countryside, or just sitting in the sun and daydreaming. Leisure is one of those qualities that has grown scarce in the affluent economy, rather to our surprise. But the answer is simple; affluence has congested our lives just as it has congested our streets.

In all societies, whether rich or poor, there is a natural tendency toward acquisitiveness, toward having more than others. The quest for wealth may be an ever present force in human nature, but it is also a disruptive force, and because of this, has been restrained by traditions and religious precepts. Greed is usually classed with dishonesty, cheating, laziness, and violence, and discouraged by gossip, ridicule, and supernatural sanctions, by suggesting, for example, that a rich man could enter heaven as easily as a camel could pass through the eye of a needle. Some of the greatest literature in the Bible is in the Sermon on the Mount where Christ inveighs against wealth—"For where your treasure is, there will your heart be also"—while pointing to the birds of the air and the lilies of the field which do not sow, reap, or spin, but yet are arrayed in greater splendor than Solomon. Since they are provided for, we too should not be concerned about food and clothing. "Seek ye first the kingdom of God and his righteousness, and all these things shall be added unto you." To want or need little is a virtue, a path to God.

The Eastern religions take this ideal of wanting less much further, and suggest that liberation is the cessation of all desire. Emerson and Thoreau were both influenced by Hinduism; Emerson's philosophy of transcendentalism is very close to it. Thoreau, knowing how practical his fellow Americans were, attempted to express the logic of reduced desire in a practical way, to show that it made life better even for selfish reasons. He suggested that happiness is the result when achievements were divided by desires, which can be expressed as:

$$\text{happiness} = \frac{\text{achievements}}{\text{desires}}$$

If one's desires are great, unhappiness and disappointment are almost inevitable since achievements are likely to fall short of them. At best, the mathematical figure for happiness would be one—if all of one's desires were achieved. But even this is rare, since desires tend to rise with achievements. The better solution is to reduce desires, since as this is done the figure for happiness rises; as desire approaches zero, a mathematician would tell us that the figure for happiness will approach infinity, regardless of what one's achievements are. In Buddhism and Hinduism, this is enlightenment, liberation, or nirvana, the goal of all life. We in the West tend to see it as the loss of will or the abnegation of life, but to have survived for thousands of years, there must be some wisdom in it that we, in our cultural youthfulness, do not yet appreciate.

Whether or not the cessation of all desire is good or not is a remote question for us, but the implications of Thoreau's equation for the consumer society are harder to disagree with. The momentum of the economy depends on unsatisfied wants, and advertising is necessary to create the dissatisfactions that keep people buying and the economy going. But the dictionary defines abundance as a "fullness to overflowing," which is "surplus to needs." *According to this definition, there is very little abundance in our society.* Few of us feel satisfied with what we have, let alone feel that we have a surplus. This is true even though in America we consume some 30 percent of the world's resources with only five percent of its population.

According to a wide body of economic research, satisfaction comes not so much from what we have, but from what we have compared to others. It is *relative income*—getting ahead of the Joneses—that gives satisfaction, but for every winner in this kind of struggle there must also be a loser. And even the winners can always find others who have more yet, which makes even the winners dissatisfied with what they have. This is the basis for the proverbial treadmill; it keeps the economy going, but it causes us to think more of what we do not have than to enjoy what we do have.

To live on less, in other words, rather than being mundane or ordinary, is actually quite extraordinary in our society, very much at odds with the mainstream pattern of behavior. And it is a brave step, since it means to move away from the "getting and spending," of Wordsworth's famous poem, by which "we lay waste our powers." Shopping is virtually a national pastime in this country, and if all of a sudden, we found ourselves unemployed or even with less income, a large void would be left in our lives. The ability to savor simple pleasures or common tasks has atrophied in the consumer society, and in this sense it is fortunate that we have so much work ahead of us because this will give us the time to develop these skills again. Hopefully, when we reach stability sometime in the dim and distant future, we will know how to enjoy it, how to relax and enjoy leisure.

Reduced Consumption and the Economy

Economists used to speak of the "fallacy of thrift," which suggested that if people saved money they might end up being poorer. This was because less spending meant fewer jobs, and with fewer people working there would be less goods produced and therefore less wealth. This "fallacy" was probably correct during the period of industrial growth when there was no need for extra savings and no shortage of raw materials, neither of which hold today. Now it would be more correct to speak of a "fallacy of profligacy," the belief that we can spend ourselves rich. But the fallacy of thrift still holds in one respect—the need for jobs. To live on less has a number of advantages for the individual, but not for the workers who are laid off as fewer goods and services are purchased. Reduced consumption strikes terror into the consumer economy, because if consumption faltered it would threaten the economy with recession or even depression.

In order to maintain balance in the economy, *it is necessary for those who consume less to produce less too*, so that an individual's consumption and production are both withdrawn from the economy, leaving the balance unchanged. This is likely to be the case in the sustainable economy anyway because the use of simpler technology and renewable resources will mean lower levels of production. Again, there should be no conflict between the sustainable economy and the mainstream economy although reduced consumption will leave some factories unused. Business leaders may speak of people's patriotic duty to consume in order to keep their plants running.

For the individual, living on less has one absolutely indisputable advantage—*the less income needed, the wider are the opportunities in the sustainable economy*. The person whose needs are few will have the freedom to choose from a wide spectrum of work in a great many locations. Those whose needs are great will be restricted to a smaller number of well-paid jobs in fewer locations, jobs for which there will be intense competition.

This is an important point, but it is not the place where many Americans are now. The hard reality for most of us is seeing paychecks fall behind inflation, and with limited options to turn this situation around. Few people find this either challenging or enjoyable. The consumer economy is now beginning to cut into us in two ways—still creating dissatisfactions but now reducing the means by which we can satisfy them—and it hurts.

"How can I cut back? I'm not making it now."

This is a familiar lament. It would seem we are all very poor. There are a good number of poor people in this country, but the average income is still an affluent one. Per capita disposable income after being corrected for inflation is still almost double what it was in 1950 (which only tells us that there are many other factors that determine the quality of life besides income). On international economic standards, even the poor in this country are quite well off, but this does not mean that being poor is not hard here; it is. But it is hard because the *relative income* of poor people is low, not because their absolute income is especially low, and also because status is so heavily based on a person's earning power in this country.

We could cut back, and cut back significantly if we were forced to by falling wages or high rates of inflation. There is much to be said for doing it voluntarily and making a positive step of it, but it will happen even if we don't want it to, even if it means that we must be pushed kicking and screaming into a simpler way of life.

But still, while it is permissible to speak in the abstract about living on less and voluntary simplicity, to speak of specifics is surprisingly difficult. It turns out to be profoundly unfashionable. It seems to be dealing in a petty and miserly way with very ordinary things. It does not sit well with the grander visions of this age, even the supposedly enlightened ones where the generous thing to do would be to help the poor, to bring them up to middle-class standards (even though to be middle class is unfashionable too). Living on less itself is said to be a middle-class concern, since the poor cannot afford it and the rich could not possibly be interested. Whatever the fashion is, it is not living on less. The simple and the down to earth do not excite us; they do not qualify as revolutionary; they are not seen as a path to liberation or freedom; the Sermon on the Mount does not speak to us. Such is the pervasive influence of the consumer society.

At any rate, the reader who is already living on little can certainly skip ahead to the next chapter, and others may wish to do so also if the material seems disagreeable. There are no spectacular new ideas or major innovations, nothing that hasn't already been written elsewhere. It is included for the reader who wishes to reduce expenditures but cannot see how it can be done, or for those who have already cut back but are looking for a few more ideas.

Food. Expenditures for food take a fourth of the typical family budget, the largest single item. Since food is a "necessity," it might be assumed that saving here would be hard, but this is not the case. It is one of the easiest. And there can be a significant by-product as well—better health. The affluent diet is not only expensive, but it has large amounts of fat, sugar, refined foods, and animal products that make it an unhealthful diet as well. There are a whole series of diseases, including diabetes, strokes, heart attacks, and many forms of cancer that are much less common or nonexistent in poorer countries, and a good part of this has to do with diet.

It has been suggested that, for both economy and health, the Chinese diet is close to the ideal. It is based on rice (although any of the grains are equally nutritious), plus large amounts of vegetables (usually cooked very lightly to preserve their flavor and food value), and with meat and fish used in modest quantities, primarily as flavoring but also to provide the small amounts of animal protein needed. In this country, grains are very inexpensive and can be used in many ways, and vegetables are a good value too, especially when grown in a backyard garden.

Such a diet might be considered an extreme way to eat in this country, but think of it as the opposite end of the spectrum from the items that loom so large in our food buying habits today, from the steak and french fries, coffee and doughnuts, the TV dinners and the soda pop diets, which are not only expensive but unhealthy as well. Any movement away from this end of the spectrum toward the grain and vegetables has two important benefits, but the immediate one is less cost. Even such things as having smaller portions of meat, for example, can make quite a bit of difference.

Time is a scarce commodity in our society, and it is one of the reasons why we use prepared foods so much. But a simple meal can be quick and easy too. It helps to cook large amounts of foods that can be used later—a supply of boiled potatoes, for example, or a pot of beans or rice, vegetables that can make a salad into a meal later, or a big soup or stew, which only needs to be reheated. Something as simple as an omelet can often be a good meal, and is quick to prepare, too.

Eating out is even more expensive than using prepared foods, and the quality, to be generous, is "mixed." It also can become quite tiring if done regularly. The way to appreciate it is to do it infrequently, and to make a special occasion out of it.

A brown bag lunch is nothing new, but it has advantages that are rarely pointed out. It takes less time to make than it takes to get served in most lunch spots during the noontime rush, and it provides the opportunity to eat outside, to go for a walk, or to read a magazine. It provides the flexibility of choosing when and where to eat, and with whom.

Housing. Housing is the second most expensive item, taking 22.5 percent of the typical family budget. Unlike food, however, housing is a difficult item to deal with for several reasons. One is related to the needs of children for safety and a good education. Another is status; the place where we live is a major way of establishing who we are in a fluid, often rootless society. And finally, housing has become tied up in all sorts of investment questions. With property values in many urban areas so high, it requires a heavy sacrifice to buy a first house. And the risk of a decline in value is now real. But continued inflation is also possible, and there is no way to know which way it will go.

One thing, however, is clear—renting has become a better value relative to buying. The cost of home ownership has gone up 254 percent since 1967 while renting has gone up only 173 percent. Renting means lower monthly costs; for many people there is no other choice. And there are other advantages as well. Problems with the plumbing or a leaking roof mean only a call to the landlord for renters, but to home owners it means bills to pay or do-it-yourself repair projects. High interest rates mean the money saved from renting earns a good return, while monthly payments are high. A rented house can generally be left on a month's notice, while selling a house when interest rates are high or prices weak can be close to an impossible task, leaving the alternatives of renting it, selling it at a lower price, or self-financing it, which means the capital is tied up and not available for other uses. The fact that the long-standing shift of population from rural to urban areas has now been reversed suggests that the demand—and the price—of urban housing will be more apt to fall than rise, another good reason to rent. Renting has plenty of its own problems, of course, but its advantages are significant as well, especially in urban areas.

One important reason for the housing shortage of recent years—and hence the high prices—is that there has been a great increase in the number of single-person households. Unmarried, divorced, or elderly individuals occupy so many dwellings that the population of a number of cities declined even though the supply of housing increased. In such a situation, doubling up makes a good deal of sense; it means cutting housing costs in half, and sharing the work of cleaning, cooking, and shopping. Elderly people especially could move into one of their houses, enjoy each other's companionship, have the revenue from the sale of the other dwelling to live on, and release a dwelling for one of the young couples who are having such a hard time finding a dwelling today. In recent decades, single persons bought houses even when they didn't need so much space because the potential for capital gains was so great. But as this potential declines, there will be less of a tendency to buy a larger house than needed.

All of these forms of sharing have their problems; living close to others always does. But in many ways these problems are human ones; to avoid them by living alone makes it increasingly difficult to ever live with someone else. Inasmuch as we are unlikely to be able to afford the degree of privacy and independence we have come to expect, the ability to get along with others will be increasingly important.

Another emerging strategy for a young couple or several individuals is to buy a rundown dwelling and build up "sweat equity" in it by rehabilitating it. This is hard work, especially as a second job after working forty hours a week, and it can take several years to finish. But if the house can be lived in while most of the work is being done, it can pay off well.

Prices for "fixer uppers" have increased along with everything else, and it is increasingly necessary to look for them in badly deteriorated neighborhoods, but if these neighborhoods are close to jobs, they should become more desirable as commuting costs go up. And the skills learned in a rehabilitation project are very valuable ones, and courses are now available to learn them.

Building a new house on your own is less frequently a possibility in urban areas for a number of reasons—few building sites, stiff building codes, vandalism on the construction site, and the high cost of borrowed money if progress is slow. In rural areas, building a new house offers fewer obstacles, especially if a trailer can be parked on the building site to live in while work proceeds. Indigenous materials can often be used, which not only reduces the cost of a house but gives it a personal touch not found in mass-produced houses.

Heating and Utilities. This is the monthly bill that is going up fastest of all, and so it is fortunate that it is one that most of us can cut back on without too much difficulty, doing ourselves and the conservation effort of the country a favor at the same time. Every bit of energy saved makes our future easier and more secure.

The quickest and easiest thing to do is to simply not heat a good part of the house, particularly the bedrooms but any other rooms that are not regularly used. For bedrooms, an electric blanket is an excellent conservation device, heating only the place where it is really needed—the bed—rather than the whole room. Most electric blankets use about as much energy as a 100-watt light bulb, and they can be turned off after the cold bed has been warmed. And without heating the whole bedroom, a window can be opened for fresh air without having to feel that expensive heat is being wasted. If someone needs to use an unheated room, the heater can be turned on. But still, one of the nice things about unheated rooms is that it draws individuals back into the warmed central living space.

On top of these "no cost" steps, there are all sorts of additional steps that take money in varying amounts—insulation, weather stripping, storm windows, day-night thermostats. The best thing about a tight, well-insulated house, beyond saving fuel, is that it is so much more comfortable, avoiding the drafts and cold spots that characterize a house that is losing a lot of heat.

Lighting is a major consumer of electricity; the expensive studies of energy used in large buildings usually end up recommending that the lights be replaced by more efficient types. Fluorescent lights are increasingly being used in homes because they use 60 percent less energy than incandescent lights, and they are becoming available in warmer colors. But simply turning off lights is again the most straightforward response. And task lighting—a small light directed on the area where light is needed—is much more efficient than lighting the whole room, and can be attractive as well.

Cleanliness is one of those things that we seem to take to extremes. The fear of harmless bacteria or the slightest odor causes us to shower daily and disinfect dishes with very hot water, while the environment is increasingly filled with unseen things that are far more dangerous. Advertising reinforces the fears we have about social acceptance and causes us to be excessively concerned about cleanliness, to make our bodies and our homes antiseptic and odorless. We could save a great deal of time, money, and hot water with more reasonable standards. Using fewer appliances would not only save on the purchase costs and the energy to operate them, but would also eliminate the hassles of keeping them going and reduce the size of the dwelling needed to house them all.

Transportation. Cars are a major expense, one for which savings are not going to come easily. Our way of life is built around cars, at least for most people, and getting by without one is very difficult.

There is one car for every 2.1 persons in the United States, which means that most families have two. It should be possible to reduce this number to one per household, saving the purchase cost plus insurance and taxes for a second car. Coordination will be required if there are several drivers, but this will mean that several tasks can often be accomplished on one trip. A number of marginal trips are likely to be skipped altogether this way, probably with few adverse effects.

Reducing the use of private cars is almost universally seen as the best way to reduce oil consumption without the loss of jobs. The new fuel-efficient cars are helping here, but there has not been a noticeable drop in the traffic on urban freeways. Car pooling is the alternative with the greatest fuel efficiency if the car is full, even higher than buses and subways. But car pooling is one of those things that people generally resist, for understandable reasons; it takes away the car's main advantages of privacy and personal convenience. Still, pooling is more attractive than buses in most sprawling American cities, and more economical as well. Buses, however, have many advantages compared to the rapid transit systems that the futurists looked forward to. First, we can afford buses since they use existing streets and can be added as the demand grows, as opposed to the huge cost of constructing subways all at once, before it is known whether they can pay their way. As more people are forced to ride buses, more routes will be established and more frequent service will be provided, and more riders will mean fewer cars on the streets to slow the movement of buses. Because buses fit so well with the decline of the automobile, they are probably the way urban transportation will go. For the individual, however, what this means is that it will be increasingly worthwhile, for both cost and convenience, to arrange one's life so that most things can be reached by walking, by riding a bicycle or moped, or by a short bus ride at most.

Clothing. The variations in the price of clothes is one of the clearest illustrations of just how important elements of status and prestige are in our buying habits. Both the better stores and the discount stores now offer clothes that are produced in Asian and East European countries and made from similar cloth. Style—and price—are the main differences. High-style clothes not only cost more but they are apt to go out of style faster. Or the attention they attract makes for overexposure after being worn just a few times. The way to discourage manufacturers from changing styles so often and spending so much on advertising is to not buy these things, not pay the premium prices that make advertising and style changes worthwhile today.

Traditional societies characteristically gravitated toward certain commonly used styles which changed very slowly, if at all. This enabled them to avoid competition over dress and made it worthwhile to use the very best materials since the garment would be worn for many years. This is the ideal—to find clothes that are comfortable and well made with the best materials, and then wear them as long as possible.

Medical Care. Expenditures for health services have increased from $12 billion in 1950, to $26.9 billion in 1960, to $286.6 billion in 1981! A good part of this striking increase is related to the growth of health programs paid for by employers or the government. As with anything for which the consumer pays less than the full costs, the tendency is to overuse the services offered. Such programs were perfectly designed by the health care industry to create demand for its services. With the medical profession deciding what treatment is necessary, it is not surprising that the frequency of surgeries, for example, is much higher in this country than in Europe.

Even though the money for these services does not come directly out of our pocket, we still pay for them, one way or another. But while health care is so organized, there is no incentive, indeed no opportunity, for individuals to reduce their own costs. How can this be changed? Already some employees are taking their benefits in cash rather than as insurance in order to increase their take-home pay. They can then buy a major medical insurance policy to take care of devastating illnesses, which costs less than full coverage, and then take steps to avoid going to the doctor for every minor thing, one of the major factors in rising medical costs.

A good medical encyclopedia or self-help book is the tool with which to do this. We often go to the doctor primarily to find out what it is that is bothering us, and whether it is serious or not. Usually it isn't, and this can often be found out quickly and easily at home with the help of a reference book. Similarly, if it is something that does need a doctor's attention, a trip to his office can be made with the knowledge that it is a necessary trip.

Not only do we go to doctors more than we should, we also take too much medicine, creating problems with side effects and even addiction. One of the most ominous problems is with antibiotics; their overuse is leading to the evolution of disease organisms that are resistant to these drugs. There is a very real danger that we may lose the benefits of these drugs when they are really needed by using them so often when they are not.

The element of medical care that is going up in cost fastest of all is hospital care, an expense that can often be reduced or even eliminated. Young couples are finding that childbirth at home with the help of a midwife can be as safe as in a hospital, and is an experience that far surpasses that in a hospital, where too often the whole process is designed for the convenience of the doctor and the hospital. At other times, hospitalization is prescribed primarily so the patient can be kept under observation by medical personnel, but with the assistance of hospital staff, this care can often be provided in the home if requested.

Dying is frequently the most expensive process of all, and a growing number of people have decided they would rather die in their own home with their family around them, and without spending months in a hospital sustained by machines and drugs, alone most of the time. Hospices are also available now where experienced personnel provide care and assistance with this often difficult process, but one that is just as much a part of life as birth, and should not be hidden behind hospital doors.

Because the medical profession has become so lucrative, it has begun to attract individuals more interested in the high income than the opportunities for service in what has traditionally been one of the finest callings. Doctors' offices increasingly seem to be run like assembly lines, impersonal and rushed, in order to process more patients. One of the best things that could happen to the medical profession would be an oversupply of doctors (that may now be emerging), which would cause a fall in the salaries doctors can command; medical students would then once again be attracted by the unsurpassed opportunities for service rather than the high incomes.

Education. A college education is becoming a dilemma in our society, partly because it is getting increasingly expensive, but also because it is becoming more and more vocational in nature while the demand for people with college degrees is weakening.

It is ironic that higher education turned toward vocational training as the country grew wealthier. It might have been expected to be just the other way, that wealth would have freed us from economic concerns and permitted education to enrich our lives. Instead, students found that if they didn't put finding a job in the forefront of their educations, they risked losing out to all the other students who did. The sad thing about many courses of study aimed at getting a good job is that they are often specialized, and if that particular skill is not needed upon graduation, the student is left with little of value after his years of study. And this is not unusual either, because fields known to have job openings attract far more students than can be absorbed and the openings are quickly flooded.

General enrichment of the mind is the surest value of formal education, as it always has been—learning how to think and to write; to appreciate the richness of the world's great literature, art, and music; the forces that shape its history; and the way the sciences help us understand the world we live in. It is such general understanding, rather than applied, that contributes most to the full life. It also contributes to society in general by providing an understanding of the broad forces that shape it. But such an education is not for everyone, and many students going to college today get very little enrichment from it. And while it would be nice to have everyone benefit from some contact with higher education, the cost can get very high. There are other places to learn about life too; experience is often the better teacher. Whether a college education is worthwhile depends almost completely on the student.

Nonnecessities. To this point, we have been dealing with what might loosely be called the necessities. I say loosely because many of them are far from necessary, things such as prepared foods, stylish clothes, a home in a better neighborhood, or a powerful, good-looking car. But beyond this category is a whole range of goods and services, often quite expensive, that can without reservation be put into the category of luxuries. These things not only are considered the best things of the affluent society, but they carry a message as well. They tell others that we have accomplished something, that we have made it. And because of this, they provide an additional element of satisfaction that is important to us.

But the cost of these luxuries can be high, and in more than just dollars and cents. They often require maintenance—a second home, a swimming pool, or a boat—which cuts into the time available to use them. Many of them necessitate travel—to the ski cabin or the condominium at the beach—which is expensive and time-consuming. And then the images on the pages of the glossy magazines often don't materialize—a vacation marred by surly hotel people or bad weather; a broken leg on a ski trip; vandalism of a vacation home; or costly repairs on a recreation vehicle. On top of this, there are always people that have even more luxuries, which generates the urge to make more money, to work harder, perhaps to go further into debt. Playing this game with gusto can generate ulcers, overuse of alcohol and tranquilizers, heart attacks and divorces, all the measures of stress in our society. And this is not just an upper-class phenomenon; anytime people strain themselves to have things beyond their means, problems are created.

Will the status symbols become more or less important as the economy slows down and incomes begin to slip? It seems like it could go either way. People could cut back on the necessities in order to continue having the luxuries which are their major source of feelings of self-worth. Or they could let the status symbols go, relieved that the deteriorating economic conditions make such strenuous expenditures out of the question. Which way it goes will probably depend on one's social environment. The mainstream economy, to the degree it remains large and impersonal, will still require some mechanism to demonstrate success, and it is hard to think of any other way this can be accomplished than the way we are familiar with today. The sustainable economy, to the degree that it can reestablish a workable community, can be expected to move toward more traditional ways of establishing status, by contributing to the community rather than taking from it by a display of wealth which makes others feel poor.

The Easy Way

Whatever one's economic situation, however, the greatest advantage of living simply is that it is so much easier. *The way to avoid stress is to leave a good margin, to live well within one's means and to stay out of debt.* This makes it possible to have the ease of mind to enjoy the good things that do not cost much—the evening with friends, enjoying one's children, listening to music, a walk in the park, working in the garden, or an evening with a good television program or a book. It means less time spent driving in traffic and looking for parking places in order to find the right product or bargains, less dealings with ill-humored salespeople, less things to fill closets and garages, to be maintained, and finally to be disposed of. The good life requires at least a degree of leisure, but just as importantly, it requires a state of mind with which to enjoy it.

To live beyond one's means is the hardest thing since it takes so much emotional energy, especially to juggle bills and payments. The debts soon run things; you become tied to their requirements. Debts make the threat of layoffs terrifying, in contrast to having savings in the bank with which to cope with lean times or to use to get started somewhere else under better circumstances. To count on a well paying job in the industrial economy is to count on a declining entity; they will exist but there will be fewer of them and they will be tough to get. To adopt a life-style based on the expectation of a high income could well mean going heavily into debt, and to be in debt is to be trapped. Savings, in contrast, provides the freedom to change when opportunities appear.

In other words, living on less has a great deal going for it, except one thing—status. It requires a high degree of self-knowledge, the knowledge of what is important to you in your life, and this can be a hard thing in a competitive society that surrounds us with all sorts of pressures to achieve so as to distinguish ourselves from the crowd. Self-knowledge requires that we sit back and ask ourselves just what it is in our life that has really given pleasure and meaning, and then to turn away from those things which have been unrewarding, regardless of the many messages the consumer economy directs at us to make us do otherwise.

Unlike Thoreau and Wordsworth, who could only rail at advancing commerce and industry, we can now relax and go along with its decline. We can move away from the strenuous excesses of our times, away from the material clutter that fills people's lives and garages, the things that go out to the garbage in big bags and cans. We can move toward some of the more universal pleasures that have been ignored because, being available to everyone, they offered no status or prestige, no opportunities to distinguish ourselves. To live on less is to have time, the ease of mind to enjoy it, and the freedom to escape, if need be, a way of life that is increasingly threatened by economic instability and the depletion of natural resources.

The pleasures and the security of the sustainable economy are increasingly real advantages, rather than impractical dreams. Living on less not only opens the door to the good life, but it is, in a real sense, a large part of the good life itself.

5
Bringing in the Boundaries

As part of the question of what is important to us, we must also ask the question, what can we affect? What is in our power to accomplish, and what is not? How can we have confidence that the work we are doing will be of lasting value, and not be washed away by the currents of change that have eroded many people's best efforts in recent years?

There are a number of important problems that insistently demand our attention: world problems of peace, economic development, and trade; national questions of economic policy, social programs, and defense; and state and local issues such as education and crime. The global village is a reality; we are all tied together now, and there is no way to turn the clock back. *But the global village is a very large one, and as we give these problems our attention, our families fall apart with painful regularity, many old people are left alone, those in need increasingly have only government to ask for help, and most disturbing of all, many children are growing up with emotional injuries that portend ill for the future.* We tend to ignore the things we can affect, the humdrum, unexciting things that are close to us, in favor of the big issues we have little control over. But it is the things that are close to us that are more likely to determine how good life is for us, and even for society as a whole in the long run.

Responsibility and the Tragedy of the Commons

There seems to be an unending stream of criticism in our society, of government and business, labor and management, rich and poor, black and white, and so on. Our large-scale society is made for this kind of talk, for blaming others for the ills of society. But *to be responsible is to be answerable for one's own actions, and it is something a society must encourage if it is not to deteriorate into a society of individuals and groups trying to take advantage of others.* To provide for responsibility is to provide a framework for the good life, to enable individuals to act constructively, to contribute to those around them and feel that it is recognized and appreciated rather than simply taken advantage of. It is much more than the punishment of criminals; it means that there is an effective mechanism for restraining those who wish to take without giving, who try to shift benefits to themselves and costs to others, and who exploit other people or the environment in a whole manner of ways, most of which violate no laws.

The fundamental nature of this problem has been described by Garrett Hardin in an influential essay published in *Science* in 1968 titled "The Tragedy of the Commons." It deals with the conditions that cause individuals, acting in their own best interests, to bring ruin to all. It does not suggest that men are basically evil, only that society must create a framework which encourages generous actions rather than selfish ones, as we do now. It deals with the necessity of restraints for the good life.

Hardin uses the common lands of England to illustrate his basic point, lands owned by everyone. During medieval times, the commons were carefully regulated to preserve their productiveness, but after these controls broke down, each farmer found himself with an incentive to graze as many animals as he could on the common pastures; if he didn't, someone else would. The result, of course, was that too many animals were grazed on the commons, and the overgrazing ruined the pasture for everyone.

Many natural resources fall under the category of common property resources—air, water, the oceans, and public lands. In order to preserve the value of these resources, their use must be controlled by the community, otherwise businessmen would keep their costs down by polluting the air and the water, the oceans would be overfished, and the public lands would be overgrazed and logged off. Always the incentive for the individual to do this is the same; "If I don't do it, someone else will, so I might as well get in and get my share while it is still possible." It forces people to think in the short term, because in the longer term the resources will be gone. Even population growth can be explained as a commons, because if one family restrains itself out of a concern for overpopulation, it will only leave more room for those who are not concerned, for those who are irresponsible. Hardin argues that to rely on conscience to control the number of children people have is to produce a society without conscience, since those without conscience will outbreed those with conscience.

Our public life has now become a commons too, with few people feeling responsibility for it, but many trying to get what they can from it. This occurs at all levels of our society, from the wealthy who contrive ways to not pay taxes to the lazy who exploit welfare, from the special interest groups who are able to gain from the treasury at the expense of others to students who do not pay off student loans. It applies to virtually everybody, in one way or another—ambitious professionals, self-seeking bureaucrats, hard-nosed labor unions, and even now the aged and the handicapped. In a sense, it is only an extension of the way our free market economy works; the opportunities are there and it is up to individuals to take advantage of them.

This situation puts a responsible person in an untenable position, one which Hardin calls the *double bind.* If he restrains himself while others do not, he feels like a fool; why should he pay all his taxes or pay back student loans if others are not? But if he joins in and exploits the potential for gain at the expense of the rest of society, he feels guilty, knowing the tragic consequences if this process went to its logical conclusion. This is the *double bind,* to feel like a fool or to feel guilty.

It is an untenable situation for society as well. It means we must rely on elaborate laws and regulations to restrain this process, but this only means the vast expansion of paperwork, bureaucracies, investigators, lawyers, accountants, police departments, and court systems. And even with all this, there are still many ways for individuals to be irresponsible, to get what they do not deserve. In such a situation, we are, in a real sense, favoring those who are the least responsible —those who do not allow guilt to interfere with what they are doing. This is the tragedy of the commons.

In a large organization—the kind most of us work in—it leads to infighting to get ahead, even if masked with civility —the persistent belittling of others' work and the building up of one's own. The alternatives here, for one caught up in such a situation, are to let others walk over you or to join the infighting. For those who have no heart for either choice, the only thing to do is to resign.

We have come to accept as normal everybody's right to get what they can from government or society as a whole, but now it is being applied to human relationships as well. Individuals take advantage of other individuals in all manner of ways, to get work or special favors that are not returned, to make sexual conquests, or to simply take from any human relationship without concern for fairness or reciprocity. Once taken advantage of, people tend to pull back and become defensive and suspicious. Even friendly contacts are treated with suspicion: "What are they really after?" It is a protective mechanism, but it undermines the basis for human relationships and contributes to the feeling of loneliness in our society. It causes people to be afraid of being too close to others for fear of being hurt. The sad thing is that both of these reactions—of the exploiter and those who are taken advantage of—*are rational responses to our situation.* It becomes hard to even imagine someone who, under such circumstances, continues to give when others only take, to be polite when others are rude, and to be cooperative when others cultivate assertiveness and intimidation.

The solution Hardin proposes to these opportunities for exploitation is *mutual coercion mutually agreed upon.* This sounds unpleasant to our modern ears, but it is essentially the traditional solution, the basis by which a community encourages responsible behavior. Those who try to take more than they give are met initially with humorous bantering, which, even though good-humored, still tells the individual that others are onto their tricks. Within a small community, this is usually effective. To preserve one's good name and the reputation of one's family is very important; it is by their good name that people are known in the community. For more serious irresponsibilities, open coercion may be necessary, or ultimately ostracism from the community, but this is rarely necessary and would suggest a serious breakdown in the community. Usually there is a strong incentive to be known as a good person, one who contributes to the well-being of the community rather than takes from it.

There is little question that these forms of "mutual coercion mutually agreed upon" work in the context of a well-established community based on widely shared values. But there is also little question that they do not work in our large, individualistic, and highly mobile society in which there is little common agreement about which actions are constructive and which are not. We all tend to rationalize whatever we are doing and are hostile toward anyone telling us what is right or wrong. We come into superficial contact with large numbers of people but have close contact with only a few. The result is a situation ripe for exploitation, one where an individual can take advantage of others in any number of ways and get away with it. More importantly, *there is virtually no way to encourage positive actions*, other than through the remnants of traditional ways which still survive—the family and those whom we feel close to—and those to whom our "reputation" is important, the modern equivalent of a "good name." And even though these close associations have been weakened in modern society, they still provide the only opportunities to avoid the tragedy of the commons.

Turning Away from the Commons

When there is no solution to a dilemma, the only response is to turn away from it, in this case to start from scratch to reestablish a moral community—one that provides a basis for responsible behavior. The government cannot do it; its scale is way too large, among many other things. The community has been allowed to atrophy in this country and is unlikely to be revived until circumstances change. The churches increasingly see faith as a private matter and speak less about trying to infuse a community with their beliefs. But some firm basis must be found to encourage the generous side of human nature rather than the selfish, a basis that is more restrictive, true, but which also offers the assurance that generosity will not be simply taken advantage of.

The logical place to start is with whatever existing relationships are available. This is most likely to be the family, but it can also be with friends or colleagues. It must be a small group, to keep the initial steps from being any more difficult than they will be anyway. It should be limited to individuals who offer a degree of continuity, since temporary associations survive only as long as individuals are getting something out of it—which too often means taking from it. Above all, it means to pull in one's boundaries, to turn away from the flattering fiction that we can affect the global village or national issues. To turn away from these exciting and important issues will be hard, but it isn't the hardest step. The hardest thing will be to make the nascent community work.

Human relations are never easy, and starting from our present situation is especially difficult because we are so defensive, so concerned about protecting ourselves and fearful of being exploited. We do not have the benefit of experience with time-tested ways or any assurance of the continuity that people in traditional society enjoyed, ways that encourage the young, for example, to honor and assist the old because they are assured of receiving the same honor and assistance when they themselves grow old. We will have to start from scratch, and it will not be easy. But we can expect that it will go better as the payoffs of the industrial economy deteriorate and a painful scarcity replaces the affluence that made the isolation and loneliness of modern life tolerable in the first place. To bring in the boundaries now not only means to enjoy the comforts of intimacy and to relearn the ways of cooperation, but also to build a human base with which to meet the future, whatever it brings.

This does not mean that we withdraw from all public life, not at all. Only that it is not the place where our emotional energy is concentrated. It simply means that we keep the unsatisfactory activities to a minimum and get through the necessary ones quickly, avoiding conflict whenever possible. It means being pleasant to those who are pleasant to us, but turning away from those who are not. It means leaving the aggressive ones to each other, to let them tear each other apart; they deserve each other. It means that we vote for the good people who are still willing to run for office, and help them resist the pressures of those who are trying to get something for nothing (which includes a good part of the general public who want lower taxes, generous programs, and a strong defense, and then to blame someone else when the budget isn't balanced). It means that we are aware of the problems in the world, but are realistic about what we can do about them. And in a fundamental sense, it means turning away from the belief that the good life can be built from the top down, through concerted political activity or major pieces of legislation. It means putting our time and our emotional energy into the human group, into the nascent moral community which will be one of the building blocks for a larger community.

To withdraw from the hectic foray of public life should not be seen as apolitical. It is simply switching to politics from the bottom up. This is the Confucian ideal as expressed in the *Great Learning* six hundred years before Christ:

> *The ancients who wished to illustrate the highest virtue throughout the empire first ordered well their own states. Wishing to order well their states, they first regulated their families. Wishing to regulate their families, they first cultivated their own selves. Wishing to cultivate their own selves, they first rectified their hearts. . . . Their hearts being rectified, their own selves were cultivated. Their own selves being cultivated, their families were regulated. Their families being regulated, their states were rightly governed. Their states being rightly governed, the whole empire was made tranquil and happy.*

How well we can "regulate" ourselves and our families is the true test of our abilities. It is far easier to blame teenage pregnancies, for example, on the existence or the absence of sex education programs in the schools than it is for parents to accept the responsibility themselves. It is easier to blame the schools for poor educational achievement although the one consistent result of research is that family background is the major determinant of educational achievement. Divorce, child beating, juvenile delinquency, and many other problems all tell us that we have not "rectified our hearts."

The Underdeveloped Countries

Responsibility in this country is one thing; we have the education, the resources, and the tools to work with, the things needed to exercise responsibility. People living in many poor countries, however, do not have the resources we have. They have made significant progress in recent years, but working against them is population growth, which threatens to outrun their efforts, speeded in places by environmental deterioration. The tragedy of the commons here is approaching a fearsome stage.

Yet again, we have to ask ourselves the question: What can we do for them that will be of value? To salve our conscience is one thing; realistic help is something else.

Several conclusions seem unavoidable. There is not the capital or the natural resources for industrialization to be the answer to the needs of the poor countries. Economic assistance is usually pictured as the generous thing to do, but it also is the one that is most flattering to us, seeing our way of life adopted by others, and is most likely to create markets for our products and military cooperation. *But given the size of the world's population and the voracious appetite for resources by the presently industrialized fraction of the world's population, the spreading of this way of life everywhere could only be temporary, at best.* At worst, it would mean the destruction of traditional cultures that are built on renewable resources, the ones which have logic for the future. It is the Western-educated elites in the Third World countries who have the most to gain from modernization, but they are also the ones most interested in the symbols of modern power, the jet aircraft, the atomic power plants, and the steel mills. We are only too happy to sell them these things, but they do precious little for the poor people who have been driven off the land, often by modern agricultural technology we have sold them—the same technology that drove so many American farmers off the land.

Most countries are getting by for the time being, even though many are accumulating debts at an alarming rate to do so. But at some stage, the following situation is likely to be encountered. A spell of bad weather leads to poor harvests, and shortages drive world food prices up. Countries that are hopelessly in debt will need large amounts of food. If the rich nations provide billions of dollars to buy what is needed, they will also drive up the prices of food for their own people. Will Americans divert very substantial sums of money from domestic needs, spend it in a way that drives food prices up, and send the food overseas, perhaps to keep starving people alive but no more able to meet the next challenge? And if we do this once, will we do it again and again as the problems worsen over the years? Can anyone envy a Congress or a president who would have to make such dreadful decisions?

But the feeling persists that there must be something we can do. We are a wealthy, powerful country, and if we really wanted to help, we could. But already, much of our help has been disruptive, even if given with the best of intentions. Health care has contributed to the problem of overpopulation, and small farmers were driven off the land because they could not compete with the low-cost food we gave or sold to them. Population control is rapidly becoming the only thing that will provide any relief from the oncoming tragedy, and although we should provide birth control materials generously, in the end we cannot make anyone use them. Responsibility is required of them too.

If it doesn't seem fair that we have so much while poor countries have so little, it should be remembered that they have things of value which we do not have. In many cases they have cultures which evolved over thousands of years, cultures that are rich in art, music, philosophy, and religious beliefs; rich in community life and the understanding of what it takes to make them work; and rich in the knowledge of how to use renewable resources to sustain human life. In many cases, these traditional societies have been weakened by modern inroads, and rapid population growth has certainly put tremendous strains on them. But the cultural resources are still there; in many cases they are what stood in the way of modernization. To be poor in these countries does not carry the stigma it does for us since most people are poor, and they have traditionally lived simply. But the kind of desperate poverty and starvation caused by overpopulation is another matter. Dealing with overpopulation is their single, overriding challenge. Our challenge is much more complex: to build a whole way of life appropriate for an era when the high-grade industrial resources have been depleted. Which will be the most difficult challenge to meet remains to be seen. Only history will tell; I would not like to place a bet either way.

The Arms Race: The Tragedy of the International Commons

This is the one we cannot turn away from; it will be with us no matter what we do. It has all the elements of a modern tragedy—the remorseless working of things—driven by the vulnerability of not arming if the other side is and the difficulty of knowing what the other side is up to, all made worse by the huge stakes involved.

But there are some favorable aspects to the situation, too, some quite important ones. The destructive power of modern weapons is so great that they have become extremely dangerous to use; the likelihood of retaliation is terribly high. And because it is necessary to be rich and powerful to participate fully in the arms race, there are only two countries that can afford it, which permits a degree of responsibility compared to a commons that is a free-for-all of many players. Nuclear proliferation works against this, but minor powers rarely have the economic strength to wage a nuclear war, and the superpowers will be careful not to let a minor power or a group of terrorists trigger a nuclear war in which the superpowers have the most to lose.

There is another factor on the side of peace—the historical experiences that have shaped the Russian mind. Just as it would be difficult to understand Americans without reference to our history and geography, it is difficult to understand the Russians without looking at the same factors. The Russians have, in a sense, an excuse for their part in the arms race, one which we chose to ignore in order to justify our part in it, to enable us to picture them as out to conquer the world. As with so much in the modern world, it is fear that is primarily responsible for what the Russians do.

The Russians have been invaded a number of times from the West, several times with great treachery and loss of life. Napoleon and Hitler both attacked even though they had signed peace treaties with Russia, and on both occasions the severe Russian winters helped defeat the invaders, but not without a terrible toll among the Russian people, who were also trying to survive the bitter cold and the destruction of war. In World War II, the Russians lost between twenty and thirty million lives, dwarfing the losses of all other countries. And for heroism, there is little that can compare with the battles of Leningrad and Stalingrad. Our freedom from Nazism in the West owes an immeasurable debt to these Russian sacrifices.

After World War II, the Russians took steps to protect themselves against being invaded by the West again. The Iron Curtain was established partly as a buffer against invading armies and partly to maintain control of countries that were seen as dangerous, primarily Germany but also its allies in World War II. Russia was also determined to develop technically, economically, and militarily, so that its backwardness would never again tempt foreign invaders. Their rapid progress in this is a great source of pride to them.

On Russia's southern flank is another source of fear, militant Islam, since some 50 million Moslems live in Soviet central Asia, and their numbers are increasing far faster than those of the European Russians. The occupation of Afghanistan, rather than being the first Russian step toward the Persian Gulf, is more likely an effort to halt the spread of militant Islam northward from Iran and Pakistan into Afghanistan, and then on into the Soviet republics to the north. European Russians are being encouraged to move to Siberia, where most Russian energy resources are, in order to not be outnumbered too badly by Moslems in this strategic region. They clearly have no desire to face in central Asia a situation similar to that in Iran. Can we say that we would feel very differently under the same circumstances?

To the east, the Russians see a billion Chinese and remember past invasions by Tartars and Mongols, sometimes forgetting that the *czar* (the Russian word for Caesar) took much of Siberia from China while trying to build a Russian empire. With hostile people on three sides, the Arctic Ocean is no more friendly on the north; icebreakers are necessary to use it for shipping even in the summer.

How different our situation is, protected by two benign oceans, bordered by smaller, friendly countries, and with little experience with foreign invaders. Is it any wonder that the Russians feel better with friendly governments on their borders and around the world (just as we do)? If they did attack the United States, imagine the problems they would face. They would have to occupy the country to stop a counterattack, but can you imagine what kind of resistance they would run into, with all the guns people have here and how much they would like to use them against occupying Russians, who cannot even control small Afghanistan?

One need only listen to the Russians' music or read their literature to know that they have much that is good. But they live in a very bleak society, one with the highest rates of suicide, alcoholism, and abortion in the world, a system that is sustained and justified in good part by fear of the West. Could it be that Soviet leaders continue to arm, knowing we will do the same, and thus help justify their oppressive control? Would peace be more of a threat to their system than any outside attack? Does our wish to "negotiate from strength" merely sustain the system we fear?

Or, we should ask ourselves, why are we so willing to spend hundreds of billions of dollars a year on defense when in the past we were isolationist, reluctant to be drawn into a war even against Hitler, who had conquered all of Europe except England? Could it be because we were self-sufficient in our material needs then, while now we must protect our sources of oil and the markets for our exports? Defense expenditures to protect the Mideastern oil fields especially could be useless since the pipelines, storage tanks, port facilities, and supertankers creeping across the ocean are vulnerable even to World War II weapons. And the Middle East is halfway across the world from us and right next door to Russia. Our real security would be better served by putting some of these billions into developing domestic energy resources and encouraging people to live on less, but this does not excite us as much as an epic struggle with the Russians.

For the time being, the arms race seems to suit Soviet and American temperaments, and the fact that both countries can afford to spend so much on arms reflects the affluence of the two countries. This is where our greatest hope lies, *because both countries are already finding it hard to fund the arms race, and as time passes, this will become more difficult yet.*

Russian problems in Poland, for example, had their origin in high food prices and shortages; if not resolved, such discontent could spread to other Russian satellites and grow to be a greater threat to Russia than attack from the West. We too may see defense expenditures as too expensive, taking too much money away from domestic programs or contributing to a federal deficit that takes capital needed by the economy. At some point, the United States and the USSR may decide that it is in their common interests to reach an arms control agreement, and reach it quickly, in order to direct their attention toward urgent domestic problems.

The same thing may be true with the exercise of political power around the world. The role of a world power was challenging to us (even if the difficulties were often frustrating), but it was by no means helpful to the rest of the world, drawing many countries into an East-West conflict they had no interest in. It caused us to support repressive governments, fearing that peasant resistance would somehow be communist, giving the communists a legitimacy they did not deserve while frustrating authentic liberation movements. Now there are huge arsenals in many countries, and just as with the guns in this country, they are a terrifying element. But overseas there is even less that we can do about them than in this country. If we feel guilty about this situation, it should be for what we have already done rather than the fact that we are able to do so little now to relieve the situation that exists. We must have faith that people will be able to work out ther own destinies. There is no other choice.

Pulling in the Boundaries Too Far: The Survivalists

The fact that a good number of Americans are buying guns, storing water and dehydrated food, and building defensible retreats in isolated areas suggests that paranoia is a force in this country as it is in Russia. The rapid growth in the survivalist industry is an ominous sign.

The worst thing about letting fear shape one's behavior is that it is, just as with the Russians, a self-fulfilling prophecy. If you are armed, your neighbors will feel they must arm themselves too. If you have food stored up with the intent of defending it rather than sharing it, it virtually forces your neighbors to do the same thing, justifying mutual hostility. Some survivalists almost seem to thrive on this hostility, and look forward to collapse and to a return to a frontier ethic with justice through the barrel of a gun, their gun.

Ironically, this Dark Age scenario is not even feasible for the survivalists. After the year's food supply is gone—assuming it was successfully defended—it would be necessary to leave the fortified stronghold to maraud for food, self-sufficiency being virtually impossible in isolated areas; that is why they are unoccupied. But marauding would be dangerous since other people have guns too. Food production would not make sense either, because it would only invite attackers. Population reduction would probably continue until a hunting and gathering level was reached, and those who survive are likely to be the most vicious killers. This is the tragedy of the commons gone the limit.

The evolution of homo sapiens has been extraordinary for one major reason—cooperation. This is what gave us our advantage over our primate relatives and led to such rapid evolution. The complexity of cooperative life and especially the need for language is the major factor that necessitated the extraordinary development of the human brain. *If we forego cooperation, we are doomed,* and pointing guns out the window is a major step in that direction.

The only way to discourage this tendency is by demonstrating the value of cooperation—that it means a congenial social life rather than a life of fearful isolation, that it means an easier life by exchanging goods rather than the back-breaking work of trying to be self-sufficient, and that it means protection too, in the unlikely event that defense is needed, of neighbors standing together. *To say that the meek shall inherit the earth is only to state a historical truth.* Unresisting India has absorbed many invaders while maintaining its cultural continuity for four millenia, while the grandeur of Rome, based on its legions and its slaves, is long since gone. All the martial empires are gone—Alexander the Great's, Napoleon's, and Hitler's—while the Catholic church survives, even without the divisions Stalin inquired about. We have inherited both elements—meekness and military ardor —and it will be a measure of our wisdom to see which we embrace as a country. For individuals, at least, the answer should be clear.

The Beacon on the Hill Grows Dim: America in Troubled Times

America offered a new beginning, a chance to start again and to avoid the wars and the corruptions of Europe. The American environment was rich and fertile, and so large that a high degree of freedom was possible. But we chose to see our success as stemming from wisdom and national character rather than open spaces and natural resources. The environment was seen as something to be "conquered," rather than a benevolent source of abundance, and we were free because of "the silken bonds of mild government," in de Crèvecoeur's phrase two hundred years ago, rather than because people were scattered thinly over a huge landscape.

The new nation gained an exaggerated view of its virtue,

an attitude that was enhanced by two world wars. Only now is this attitude beginning to weaken as abundance wears thin and we begin to face that element that other countries have always faced—limited resources. It is apt to be a humbling experience, and not an easy one for us to cope with. There are likely to be larger political swings as we try one approach after another to reestablish the economic and political power we once had. The trend toward one-term presidents may continue until we cease asking presidents to do an impossible job—recreate abundance and the military power that went with it.

America, a beacon on the hill, a light to the world! It was a grand vision, and it is never pleasant to see a grand vision dim. It leaves a hollow feeling, of missed opportunity, of failure. But just as we should not have claimed so much credit for our successes, so we should not blame ourselves too much for the decline. It was inevitable, sooner or later. If not energy now, it would have been something else later—excessive scale of technology, poisons in the environment, or any number of the social pathologies. In a real sense, our problems now are a direct result of our success in the past—our economic vitality and our technological advances. It is better that the task of building a sustainable way of life begin now rather than trying to delay it—which is what we hope for when we try to revitalize the industrial economy.

What is needed is a new vision, one that is capable of moving people yet respects the more universal qualities of human existence, especially the need to live and work together within the constraints of nature. Americans frequently argue that to live simply is not a powerful enough vision, that it cannot compete with the dynamism of American society and our urge to achieve, but this is only to restate the dilemma; this is the vision that is now dimming as exaggerated expectations run headfirst into barriers of all sorts—scarcities, high interest rates, debts, inflation, and falling incomes.

Rather than a single vision, in fact, we are more likely to see a series of different visions emerge across the country as new ways of life are developed. We are building from the ground up, and the visions that work—those that set patterns others follow—will be the ones that successfully deal with the realities we face.

6
Roles

Every society depends on roles, on set ways of behavior that are expected of individuals in different positions. Roles are a cultural universal—they are found in all societies—and this is almost certain to remain so, whether we like them or not. Roles are simply too useful to do without.

Roles make our world manageable and understandable. It is through roles that we know what to expect from people we come into contact with daily—teachers, police, clergy, salesclerks, and neighbors. With well-established roles, people can be counted on to act in expected ways; it is comforting to know that teachers will not try to force their political beliefs on our children, that the clergy will support our most cherished values, that neighbors can be counted on to help when we need them, and that the police will respond to our calls for assistance. It is through roles that we know people, and through roles that people become a source of comfort and security. In a real sense, roles help knit together the frail thing that is society, to protect it from chaos and anarchy.

But in our society the individual has come to be the measure of all things, and it is not surprising that roles have been widely criticized. They are pictured as undemocratic, as keeping people in limiting and demeaning ways that are, at best, arbitrary and unnecessary, and, at worst, a way for "the system" to hold people down and deny them their chance to exercise their full potential. When an increasing number of people no longer accept the idea of roles and instead demand the freedom to be their "true selves," it creates real problems. It leads to the fear that schools, workplaces, churches, public parks, and our neighborhoods may be working against us. Uncertainty replaces the confidence with which people can meet the world they live in. These fears cause people to retreat from public involvements, but then the deterioration in roles infects the closest relationships too, between husband and wife, parent and child. The breakdown in roles contributes to the feeling that there is little left that can be counted on, that can be trusted. There seems to be no refuge.

There are problems with roles today, there is no question of that. But rather than seeing them as problems with the concept of roles, they should be seen as problems in our society, especially as a result of a period of rapid changes that destroyed many roles and weakened others. To reject roles is to forego a device that almost certainly developed along with the earliest human groups hundreds of thousands of years ago; homo sapiens have always been a sociable species, living in groups rather than as solitary individuals. The task is not to perfect our "modern consciousness" so that we can achieve full autonomy and transcend the need for roles; that denies our social natures and the interdependencies in all societies. No, the task is more down to earth—to learn how to use roles well, how to use them so they contribute to a comfortable and satisfying way of life, not unduly constraining people, but not leaving them rootless and insecure either. As always, balance is the goal. To find it, it is necessary to have some feeling for the age-old functions of roles, and why it is that the deterioration of roles in the modern era has taken a good deal of pleasure out of life.

Synergism, The Foremost Function of Roles

When two or more individuals, working together, achieve an effect that each, working alone, is incapable of, it is termed *synergism*. It is an excellent thing, and was especially valued when resources were limited and human muscles did most of the work.

But we haven't had these restraints for some time now. We have been able to afford the luxury of individualism, which made working with others seem a waste of time, conjuring up images of committee work, disagreements, and bureaucracy, and interfering with our own work, which was more important. We are told time and time again that nothing worthwhile is accomplished except by individuals. A good many people going back to the land are doing so to avoid dealing with people (initially at least, until they discover how much work self-sufficiency is). But our obsession with ourselves and our dislike of having to work with others will very soon become a luxury we can ill afford. As scarcity comes to characterize our world more and more, we will rediscover how roles make life easier; either that or we will find our lives unnecessarily impoverished.

Folk societies prescribe roles in elaborate detail, and there are a number of functional reasons for doing this. If done satisfactorily, roles divide up the work that needs to be done, allocating agreeable and disagreeable duties alike. Roles were never meant to be equal; some were more desirable and carried more status than others. *But all conferred honor in their fulfillment.* Each person could be proud of his or her role, no matter how modest, and people could be assured that they had something of value to hand down to their children. Roles encouraged responsibility too, since tasks were clearly defined, and if they didn't get done, it was difficult to shift the blame to others. But roles also placed limits on one's responsibility, and once accomplished a person could relax, knowing his work was done; teachers did not have to be parents to neglected or abused children, and mothers did not have to have careers in order to be respected. Roles were arranged to be manageable; an ordinary person could handle them, and enjoy the sense of accomplishment that went with them. Roles restricted upward mobility, true, but they also assured a person's usefulness and provided a sense of identity, of who they were in a community.

We, in contrast, denigrate roles and are unwilling to honor those who carry them out faithfully. We see nothing "creative" in following established ways, especially compared to the accomplishments of the superachievers that we are fascinated with. It takes a good deal of wisdom and self-knowledge to be proud of the very significant achievement of being a good parent, for example, when society seems not to notice it, or to do a job well that society ascribes little value to beyond a paycheck. Without roles and the limits they prescribe, there is always more that we could be doing and higher things to aim for, which makes it very difficult to relax with a mind at ease, to enjoy a fine day, the sound of children's voices, or a period of contemplation. We have too much on our minds; we have things we want to do; we have rising expectations. And while it is nice to have the freedom to move as high as our abilities can take us, it is not so nice to have only ourselves to blame if we fall downward. Failure is the other side of success in our society, and it hurts. It is common, too, because rather than being content with what we have accomplished, we think about what we have not been able to do. Roles would discourage us from our tendency to aim too high and try for too much.

Traditional roles can perhaps best be thought of as part of a complex game, the rules of which, taken together, form a culture—a way of life. Without the rules, there is no game. Fortunately, we have held on to a fair number of these rules, but just losing as many as we have means that many individuals find themselves at loose ends in a very big society without satisfactory outlets for their energies, wanting to do something worthwhile, to gain acceptance and respect, but unable to find a way to do it, unable to find a niche where they fit. In today's society, we are supposed to create our own roles, but the most common result is that people do not know who they are, and end up instead trying to emulate someone else or the members of a group they would like to be a part of. We tend to think that inside of us there is a true personality, which is perhaps correct. But if so, this personality is a product not only of our genetic makeup but our life experiences as well, of genes and environment, of nature and nurture. If we deny external influences on our personality we may, in the process, be creating the bland, colorless figures so common today, in contrast to the vivid characters common in traditional societies.

The economy, if not the "only game in town," is certainly a very important game to us, and it is one in which the rules are known. But its rules are those of the impersonal market, a highly competitive game that uses natural resources out of all proportion to the returns generated. This is doing little with much. Traditional societies did not have the technology or the resources to do this. They had no choice but to try to do much with little. And when they were able to accomplish more working together than they could working alone, that was synergism. It was a fine achievement.

The Second Function of Roles—Conflict Avoidance

Synergism is the creative side of roles, of providing for the material needs of society efficiently as well as in an emotionally satisfying way. The evolution of roles, however, probably came more from the effort to avoid conflict than it did from a conscious effort to achieve a synergistic effect.

Roles reflect a realistic assessment of human nature. Rather than expecting that people will be able to discuss their differences, understand why others act as they do, and reach some resolution that is satisfactory to all, our ancestors simply defined roles to avoid conflicts in the first place. After all, there are some tasks that nobody wants to do; roles reduce the argument and the manipulation that would inevitably occur if every job had to be decided on the basis of discussion, with individuals trying to shed the unpleasant tasks or obtain the profitable and pleasant ones. Roles can never eliminate conflict, but each one that removes a source of contention smooths out human relationships.

The market economy operates on the principle that anything that interferes with the free play of the market, such as roles, is wrong. Roles reduce competition, the motive force in the market economy. Our economic system can be seen, in fact, as a huge arena for controlled conflict, and the fact that this conflict has been safely contained is a significant achievement. But it is conflict just the same, and most cultures have tried to avoid conflict, or at least reduce it as much as possible, seeing cooperation as far more desirable. Roles are a part of this ongoing effort, while at the same time dividing up the work as well as possible and giving individuals honor for doing their share. In traditional cultures, the competitive impulses are restrained as vigorously as we stimulate them in our society.

In hunting and gathering societies, for example, the hunting is almost invariably done by men while women do the gathering. The origins of this role separation are lost in the past, and while there are physiological differences that suggest the different roles—especially childbearing by women—these differences cannot explain the extent to which role separation between men and women is carried. They are often supported by quite powerful religious beliefs; for example, the Eskimos believed that the animals they hunted would be offended if they were hunted by a woman and would leave the area. It would seem that there must be something functional about this role separation, since it is found in such widely different environments and is so rigidly adhered to.

The answer must be cultural; clear role separation reduced conflict. Roles contributed to the partnership between men and women that was so necessary if hunters and gatherers were to survive. The sexes could not afford the luxury of competing together as we can, and the physiological differences between men and women were enough to tip the roles in the direction of men hunting and women gathering.

In the medieval era, guilds dominated the economic activity of the towns and cities, regulating every aspect of each craft—the materials used, the quality of workmanship, and the wages paid apprentices. The guilds were approved by the church in return for acceptance of the concept of the just price for the product sold, a price that was adequate for a reasonable income but not more. The entire system was based on the restraint of competition—the security of each craft and the requirement to serve the needs of the public with assured quality at acceptable prices.

Perhaps the most extreme definition of roles is the caste system in India. Caste is at the heart of Hinduism, since the caste a person is born into is believed to be based on the quality of his previous life. How well people live their lives determines whether their next reincarnations will be in a higher caste or a lower one. For a Hindu to try to transcend the caste he is born into would be to cheat in this particular game, to try to deny one's former existence. The contemplative element in Indian civilization and its incredibly rich religious life is very much a part of the caste system, because people's minds are turned from worldly ambition to seeking advance through spiritual perfection instead. Caste is an important rule in the game of life that is the culture of India, just as individual achievement and the downplaying of roles is an important rule in our game. *Both are extremes*, but on the opposite ends of the spectrum.

All societies establish "role models," ideal figures on which individuals can pattern their own behavior. During medieval times, there were patron saints for each craft, for members of a family, and even for animals to encourage kindness toward them. Mary was venerated as the always tender and forgiving ideal of motherhood. Stories were told that illustrated proper behavior of children, the obligations of kindness and charity, and gave direct meaning to the dangers of the seven deadly sins—pride, lust, envy, anger, covetousness, gluttony, and sloth. Behavior was everywhere prescribed, but for the purpose of facilitating the progression of life, to make it agreeable and to reduce the conflict that could tear it apart if allowed to. The word tradition stems from the Latin word *traditio*, meaning to transmit or hand down—to preserve the strategies that evolved over the years to cope with the not insignificant problems inherent in human nature.

Not all societies were successful in their role making. Some roles became cultural dead ends, traps that sustained conflict, by requiring the killing of an enemy to gain manhood, for example, or a machismo that required that women be treated as children. Some roles became too powerful; military leaders became warlords, and priests gained control of people through fear and superstition. Even where roles were successful, it was too much to hope that every individual would fit into the roles they found themselves in. A good society was one that provided alternatives for those whose roles were uncongenial to their nature and talents, outlets that ranged from a remote monastery to a university in the capital city, from being a shepherd immersed in nature to being immersed in the throbbing life of a great city, from joining the military to being a trader in distant lands.

Sometimes roles grew excessively rigid, so that societies became unable to adjust to changes they encountered. This could happen to us, even though we resist roles, if our behavior is too fixed in other ways. We too could fall into a cultural trap if we make virtues of some of our sicknesses, such as seeing cooperation and compromise as weaknesses, and autonomy as strength.

Signs of the Times; Men and Women

Ah, love, let us be true
To one another! for the world . . .
. . . .
Hath really neither joy, nor love, nor light,

Nor certitude, nor peace, nor help for pain;
And we are here as on a darkling plain
Swept with confused alarms of struggle and flight,
Where ignorant armies clash by night.
From "Dover Beach," MATTHEW ARNOLD

Arnold wrote his famous poem in the middle of the last century when the tumult of history was rising to the crescendo of the twentieth century. His plea, that men and women hold to each other through it all and together be as a refuge from the struggle and pain, has unfortunately been disappointed. In retrospect, this was probably inevitable; it is rare for any part of life to stand apart from the rest. Rather than being true to one another, we have instead too often been true to ourselves first. That is the message our world increasingly conveyed to us, and not surprisingly, relations between men and women grew prickly and difficult.

We must not exaggerate the problem, as it seems the media does, but neither should we deny that divorce rates are high and many men and women have chosen to live alone, as more tolerable than living with a partner. Fidelity and shared trust are still a great source of joy, but they seem difficult for us to find. All too often what appears to be an ideal marriage breaks down in bitterness and hostility in the divorce courts, harming children as well as parents. Relations between the sexes have become another source of pain in a world that already has more than enough of it.

No one with his eyes open can fail to be sympathetic to the plight of women today. Their traditional functions, of childbearing, nurture, and care of the family have been diminished as families grew smaller, schools became more important in education, and goods and services formerly provided in the home became available in the marketplace. The suburban home, with all its space and laborsaving devices, only served to isolate women further and to trivialize many of the tasks that were left. At the same time, men's role of breadwinner was expanding beyond all recognition in response to the heady opportunities available in the economy, opportunities that drew men's emotional energy away from the family and into a single-minded effort to succeed. But when women tried to enter the work force, men were, not surprisingly, less than enthusiastic about it; the always frail male ego was threatened more by women than it already was by men in a dynamic, rapidly changing economy, and with less need for human muscles, there was little doubt that women would be effective competition. At the same time, our obsession with economic success meant that we inadvertently belittled women who stayed in the home, as "only" housewives. The imbalance and unfairness in this situation quickly generated hostility toward men as well as to the concept of roles, which came to be seen as the instrument by which men kept women in their unsatisfactory situation. Men seemed to have all the good things while women were left with little.

A good part of the problems of the modern era, in fact, can be interpreted as stemming from its almost obsessive masculinity. Aggressiveness and the urge to achieve, which in the past were restrained and redirected into more generous pursuits, have in our times not only been released, but raised to an exalted position. They have found outlets in all sorts of unsavory places, in colonial empires, world wars, political ambition, and in "going for the gold," with anything less meaning virtually nothing. Such masculine behavior made sense in the evolution of our primate ancestors; defending the band and fighting for the right to mate with as many females as possible contributed to the survival of the fittest, but as cooperation grew increasingly important, these masculine qualities were discouraged. Now they are being released again, and we are learning how disruptive they can be. We are learning how vulnerable masculinity is to doubt and failure, and how it seems to need to continually assert itself to demonstrate its mastery.

The terms *masculine* and *feminine* inevitably bring up the question of what these terms mean. The charge is that they have been defined in arbitrary and incorrect ways in order to keep women in a subordinate position. It is true that much of what is deemed masculine and feminine is culturally defined, as illustrated by the great diversity of behavior worldwide. But there are a number of differences that go beyond culture. A recent study, *Human Sex Differences: A Primatologist's Perspective*, by G. Mitchell, summarizes these differences, in humans as well as in the primates, our closest animal relatives. *When differences between the sexes are found in all human societies and in the primates as well, then it can be assumed that the source is in genetics rather than culture.* The differences are interesting.

There are of course the obvious ones—the ability of females to bear children and the greater size and strength of the males—the differences that have been reduced in importance by smaller families, modern machines, and sophisticated weapons. But there are behavioral differences as well. Males are more aggressive than females in all groups, a difference that begins early—at two and a half years for humans—and continues throughout life. In all cases, females are more centripetal; they are more inward looking, more socially centered, and more concerned about reducing social tensions. Males are more peripheral; they explore away from the group more, are more venturesome, and more public about their actions. Females are more intimate; they stand closer to others, have more physical contact, look at each other directly in the eye more often, and in humans, disclose more about themselves when talking than men do. These differences are reflected in the tasks males and females excel in. Males are more competent in visual and quantitative tasks, while females do better in close visual and verbal tasks.

Research with humans can, of course, be taken much further than with primates; in the games researchers set up to observe differences in behavior, the results are again consistent with common conceptions of what is masculine and feminine. Mitchell does not argue in support of roles; just the opposite, in fact. But still he concludes:

> *Data such as the above do not lead us to believe that men are simply dominating submissive women who, in turn, are simply more compliant than the men. Things are more complex than that. Men and women have different objectives. Men want to win; women want to establish social relationships. (p. 113)*

Both male and female behavior were formed in the crucible of evolutionary survival, and even if the demands are different now, we still have the genes that were shaped by this process. It is not that we have no power to resist nature; culture has long done this with the control of sex, for example, replacing the free-for-all of males fighting to mate with females with all sorts of taboos and restrictions. Freud was correct; culture does repress human instincts, and in so doing creates all sorts of neuroses. But with sex, at least, this was absolutely essential; it is what made the family and society cooperative units and permitted human society to advance rapidly, leaving our primate ancestors behind. Cooperation paid off spectacularly compared to competition; we succeeded, it is said, because we escaped from our "selfish genes." As already mentioned, the evolution of speech and the rapid growth of the human brain were made necessary, in large part, by the demands of cooperation.

If we really worked at it, we might be able to eliminate "sexual stereotypes," but for what purpose? Are we to discourage feminine qualities that are so important as our world grows crowded and replace them with masculine ways? The feminine qualities of nurture, emotional support, and intimacy are ones that our society desperately needs. It was these feminine qualities that in the past were so appreciated —the selflessness of a wife or mother who devoted herself to the well-being of her family and those around her. If selfless activity is the surest source of happiness, as the world's universal faiths contend, then it would follow that *the traditional role of women was the more personally satisfying as well as being so valued by society. But instead of encouraging the feminine, we belittle it as weak and passive, while offering all manner of incentives to masculine behavior.*

In our present situation masculine patterns of behavior are in a very real sense pathological; the life expectancy of a man today is *eight years* less than a woman's, a difference that was only two years at the start of this century (about what it is in traditional societies). The earlier deaths of men can be attributed partly to smoking, but this is part of the masculine pattern that women are picking up, along with higher crime rates, increased suicide, and other masculine pathologies. Women have indeed "come a long way," but they still have a long way to go to catch up with men. The imbalance in masculine and feminine roles has contributed in large measure to our society becoming a colder and less comfortable place to live in.

Why do we continue to push women in the masculine direction? Are we so obsessed with aggressiveness and achievement that we must denigrate the role that encourages intimacy and human relationships? Are we to destroy the natural complementarity between men and women, of provider and sustainer, and to make them autonomous competitors instead? If human evolution is seen as demonstrating the value of cooperation, what is to be gained by reverting back to the competitiveness of the primates? *To destroy the feminine could well be the supreme example of destructiveness in an era that has already destroyed so much of value.*

Fortunately, this is unlikely. Not only is it very difficult to go against the grain of nature this way, but there are way too many satisfactions in the differences between men and women and their complementarity within the family. The family is still the strongest and best part of our lives today, as we will see in the next chapter, and reproduction is still a biological process supported by all manner of instincts. And this era, which has afflicted men, women, and the family so painfully, will not last forever; already there are signs that the excesses are abating. Many women are looking at careers more realistically, and learning how to enjoy getting out in the world and earning some income without sacrificing the pleasures and satisfaction of having children or the well-being of their children. Yet the ways of doing this, such as part-time work and waiting until children are well along before beginning a career, are not totally satisfactory either. It is in the sustainable economy that the conflicts will fall away more rapidly, an economy where husbands and wives pull together in the same direction rather than in different directions. When cooperation is necessary to make a family enterprise work, then we will be in the situation where our evolutionary heritage will be useful once again, where cooperation becomes the bond that holds men and women together and generates trust and fidelity. It is when two people need each other that love and being true to each other becomes a natural thing, and brings the joy and peace and certitude that Arnold yearned for.

Scarcity and the Reemergence of Roles

Alvin Toffler wrote *Future Shock* in 1969 when oil was still $3 a barrel; there seemed to be nothing that could stand in the way of technological advance and the accelerating rate of change which he foresaw. But the new technology to power these changes has been uncharacteristically stingy with its benefits, especially where we need it most, in providing new energy sources. Those individuals whom Toffler saw as best suited for the future—who thrive on a steady stream of change—must now adjust to life without a new job every few years, a new family arrangement, a new kind of therapy, or a new drug experience.

Scarcity offers to save us from our excesses, but it will not be easy, simply because we have been shaped by the excesses of this age. Our history may not be much help either, especially as it is seen by politicians and businessmen who make it a paean to the pioneer and the hardy individualist. But the vast majority of lives through our past were spent enmeshed in human relationships, in barn raisings, husking bees, election day picnics, church socials, union meetings, trade associations, clubs, town meetings, and family gatherings. These activities did not make much impact on the history books, but they touched our lives more than those of Stonewall Jackson and J. P. Morgan. Our national experience has almost anything that we choose to draw on.

For the time being, we have a rather unusual situation. Even though there are few people who are willing to defend roles, many support them with their actions. The excesses of masculine roles seems to have created a reaction among men —who are increasingly interested in the pleasure of their homes and families, and among women—who are seeing their choices more realistically. And the chaos in roles today has at least one advantage; it facilitates adaptation to changing conditions. Scarcity may present some unusual problems for us to cope with, especially if it comes on abruptly, and a willingness to take on unconventional roles may be quite important.

During this process, however, it will be important to remember the age-old reasons for roles—to facilitate synergism and avoid conflict, to make it easier for people to live and work together. There should be no hesitation to define roles, not rigidly in these fluid times, but as the need becomes apparent. *And the goal should be to design roles that are satisfying to us and which make life around us better; that is the real challenge to our humanity and our creativity.* To resist roles, for any reason, is to forego an extremely useful tool, one that is almost certainly essential for the good life. To reject them means to try to do things the hard way and thereby jeopardize the success of an otherwise hopeful venture.

But we shouldn't exaggerate the problems either, especially between men and women; the family is doing quite well.

7
The Family

The family is the best part of life today. That is a fact, if we can believe the pollsters. A Gallup poll taken in 1977 found that a larger percentage of Americans are highly satisfied with their family life, 79 percent, than any other item they were asked about, including satisfaction with their life overall (69 percent), this country as a place to live (57 percent), their work (49 percent), or the lowest item, the way democracy is working in this country (32 percent). If this is the case, why do we persist in seeing the family as falling apart?

The family is under stress in our society, there is no question of that. But just as assuredly, the family is resilient and adaptable; it is a survivor. Even with all the things our society does to undermine it, inadvertently or not, the family is still the strongest element of our society. The *95 million* husbands and wives living together dwarf the *17 million* adults living alone. and 40 percent of the people living alone are women over fifty-five, mostly women who have outlived their husbands. High divorce rates suggest people are leaving marriage in droves, but the high rate of remarriage for divorced people also suggests they want to forego their state of individual freedom. And the high rates of failure in these remarriages suggest that *it is the individuals who are not up to being married, rather than marriage being obsolete.* To make a family work takes a degree of maturity and cooperation, which our society does not tend to encourage.

But for those who can make a family work, it offers a number of protections against the stresses of modern life. Married people live longer, are happier, and earn higher incomes than unmarried people. Men especially benefit from being married. Divorced men have death rates 3.4 times higher than married men, are 8.8 times more apt to die of cirrhosis of the liver—suggesting alcoholism, 4.7 times more likely to commit suicide, and 7.5 times more apt to be homicide victims. Men who have never married are not the dashing singles so often pictured in the media; they are far more likely to be in prison, to be alcoholic, or to be in poor health. They earn incomes well below married men, roughly comparable to what women and black men earn, two groups generally considered to be discriminated against in the job market. And although women are able to cope with being alone better than men, they too have higher mortality rates when living alone than when married. Married people describe themselves as being happier than unmarried people; 45 percent of married people say they are very happy, while only 33 percent of unmarried people do. Again, the insistent question comes back: Why does our society feel the need to picture married life as oppressive, and to virtually ignore the family except to chronicle its demise? It is a disturbing question.

The family's function is too important for any society to get along without. Biological reproduction is only half of it, the easier half too since both men and women have more than enough sexual instincts to assure the replacement of the species (too much, perhaps, in this era of overpopulation). The more critical function of the family today is *social reproduction,* bringing up children to be good members of a society and capable of sustaining it from one generation to the next. When the family falters in this task, the entire fabric of a society is endangered, for if the family does not do its job here, the government certainly cannot do it in the family's stead; this is one thing we have learned in recent years. There is little question that the large number of injured young people in foster homes, mental institutions, or correctional institutions would be far, far better off in a solid family situation, thus avoiding the necessity of these expensive and usually ineffective programs. When damage is done to young people in their early years, it is very hard to repair, and the need for many social welfare programs today is a measure of the failures in families in recent years. It also suggests how much we owe to the large number of people who have made their families work, and who have produced good young people under difficult circumstances.

Family, Past and Present

The modern era was in no way planned to be an attack on the family: just the opposite, in fact. Affluence was to remove the toil that oppressed the family in the past, and replace it with the leisure and the comforts to permit individuals to grow in a stable, supportive situation. But as with so many expectations of what affluence would bring, this is not the way it worked out. Just as affluence did not cause us to beautify our cities, to eliminate poverty and ignorance, or provide for the leisurely enjoyment of the arts, literature, and philosophy, so it did not strengthen the family. It is interesting, and surprising in a way, how many of the fruits of affluence either turned out to taste bitter or simply did not materialize at all.

Affluence and individualism, two factors that characterize our age, worked directly against the family. Affluence permitted each member of the family to be independent of the others, each child with his or her own room, television, telephone, and later on, car. When each member had his own job, the pattern was complete. The home was the place where they met at mealtime, if their schedules conformed, and where they could argue about who should do the unrewarding maintenance tasks that were still required. If something went sour, there was less incentive to work it out; individual members had the capacity to go their own way. The family was no longer the center of life; the action was in the economy, in the schools, or in a vast number of social activities. For a while, our society toyed with the fantasy that the individual was strong enough to do without the family altogether. It was flattering, in a way, to think that we did not need this petty institution, with all its petty squabbling and petty demands. The world was too big for all that.

How different it was in the past (and, in all likelihood, the future). Without affluence or so many forms of government assistance, it was essential that the family unit work, and work well. The family made a substantial difference in the quality of life; a single person was rarely able to sustain a household, and usually had to live in a boarding house or take work as a hired hand, maid, or servant in return for board and room and a small salary. Men were required to prove that they could support a wife before gaining the permission to marry, by paying a bride price, mastering a trade, or owning land or sufficient numbers of animals. The control of marriage permitted a degree of control over reproduction, and gave society some assurance that parents would have the capacity to provide for their children. The economic importance of the family helped shape it into a cohesive unit and gave the family the power to reconcile differences, to cause its members to work together, and to generate loyalty and confidence. These loyalties were what assured family members of emotional support and gave them a feeling of their place in the scheme of things.

In simpler times, without all the diversions we have now, children were one of the greatest joys in life. *Which of the pleasures we fitfully seek today provide satisfactions comparable to the pleasures of children?* We tend to see large families in the past as stemming from the need for many hands to help with the work, but this reason for large families is generally exaggerated; to bear, nurture, and sustain children for some two decades is a rather high price to pay for the relatively few years of work during which each child is full-bodied and able to provide a significant amount of help before going off to form their own household, something parents are often obligated to help with also. If there is an economic logic for large families, it is that children act as a form of social security for the parent's old age. But there is no way to distinguish this from the primary benefit of a large family—the pleasure of being surrounded by children, grandchildren, brothers and sisters, nephews and nieces all during one's life but especially in old age. Peter Laslett, in describing preindustrial England in *The World Which We Have Lost*, describes a society dominated by the family. "Time was when the whole of life went forward in the family, in a circle of loved, familiar faces, known and fondled objects, all scaled to human size. That time has gone forever. It makes us very different from our ancestors."

A world built around the family was not utopian by any means; the family is a microcosm of the larger society, a stage to play out conflicts and struggles, many of which we now play out on a larger stage. But the family offered a more satisfactory place for this, one that encouraged cooperation and mutual support rather than competition and calculation of individual gain. The family reflects the central role of cooperation in our evolutionary makeup and the emotional obligations of blood ties, all in clear opposition to the autonomous and combative individual. The family provides a secure base from which individuals can venture out into the larger world and test their powers without having to fear risking everything; the family was there to fall back on if things did not work out.

The extended family meant that there was a larger base for this security since kin could be counted on to help a family through a lean time. Wider ties also meant that the responsibility for raising children was not concentrated so heavily on two parents. Relatives, neighbors, shopkeepers, and church people all could be counted on to reinforce the parent's task, and do their share in having young people grow up in such a way that they would contribute to the common well-being and be good parents themselves. This took a good deal of the pressures off the parents, exchanging it for obligations to do the same thing for others over the years. Children grew up feeling that their behavior was not a matter for them alone, but was important to the entire community.

Without this reinforcement, we are asking much more of two parents when we ask them to create the conditions in which their children can grow into healthy, responsible individuals. A great deal of conflict is concentrated in this very small group—all the age-old difficulties of making a family work plus now the conflicting demands of the larger society, a society which calls for all sorts of things that are at odds with the interests of the family and which gives it little honor and encouragement. Still, even in the poorest, most crime-ridden neighborhoods, the youngsters that grow strong are usually those with a strong family behind them. Time and again, it is a parent or a relative they talk about who made all the difference in the direction they took.

The fact that society is changing so rapidly makes it difficult for parents to rely on their own childhood experiences as a guide to raising children. Each of us is shaped by the world we grew up in—the Roaring Twenties, the Depression, World War II, the affluent postwar years—which means that different generations have different values. This generation gap often separates parents and their children, causing parents to be disappointed with what their children do and children to feel their parents are hostile or unsympathetic to the things being asked of them outside the home. The parents either have to harp on things they do not like to see in their children or let them go on, tacitly approving them with their silence, both of which tend to frustrate parents' generous wishes for their children. Children, too, are caught between conflicting urges, either feeling guilty at going against their parents or feeling put-upon if they go along with their parents' wishes. The double bind even afflicts children in our society.

The absence of both continuity between the generations and certainty in the values to be instilled makes raising children much more difficult today than in the past. And because of these real difficulties there are many professionals offering help. But too often this help only further weakens the confidence which parents must have to raise their children well, and makes their job more difficult rather than easier. Professional counselors, whether in private practice or with the government, inevitably feel the urge to prove the value of their services, and their tendency is to suggest that if parents look to their own instincts or rely on their common sense they will do the wrong things, perhaps injuring their child. And it is not that professionals have that good a record; they are often able to help, but they also get caught up in trying to prove their own ideas or become involved in movements that are more important to their professional career than they are to parents. And many turn out to be wrong; think of all the problems caused in the past by rigid feeding schedules and toilet training, which were deemed to be essential for discipline, and in recent years by the rejection of all discipline, which was very attractive to parents who did not have confidence in their ability to discipline their children. They were more than happy to stand back and allow their children to develop "naturally"; this was an easy philosophy to "sell," and as with any commodity, when there are ready buyers, there will be someone around to sell it.

Disagreement over how to raise children is one of the many factors that contributes to divorce, and tensions, arguments, and divorce proceedings are powerful forces on children caught up in them. A study by the Survey Research Center at the University of Michigan found that many years later the young adults that came from broken homes were more apt to describe themselves as less happy and in poorer health than others, with more anxieties, less self-esteem, closer to a nervous breakdown, and to think of their childhood as the most unhappy time of their lives. They were also more apt to have marital problems themselves, and to be less involved with their children. To love is to risk, and hard experiences makes it difficult to take the risks. In a very real sense, the "sins" of the parents are visited upon their children.

It seems characteristic of the modern temperament to believe that it is possible to have the benefits of a marriage without giving up the pleasures of being single. To this way of thinking, there is nothing served by limiting sexual relations to the same person for years and years; both partners should be able to enjoy the spice of sex with other partners off and on. This has a superficial logic to it, but it doesn't work. Being single and being married are two different stages of life and call for different kinds of behavior. Both should be savored for what they have to offer, and ideally a person should outgrow the stage of singleness before deciding to get married. Those who do not feel this should probably not get married, and certainly should not have children. In a sense, to remain single all through life is to be modern—to be immersed in loyalties to oneself, to "getting the most out of life," and to cutting off relationships with others as soon as they are no longer enjoyable. This too has a superficial logic to it, but it doesn't work out that way; the family turns out to be the more satisfying way, assuming we can believe the polls, even with all the difficulties of sustaining long-term relationships.

There are a number of problems in the family today, including some nasty ones such as child abuse, incest, wife beating, and spouses murdering each other. There are predictions that the family is finished, that it is simply a hangover from the past, and that its decline will continue. These predictions are absurd. The family has changed in recent decades, of course, but it still provides a core of continuity which is stronger than the external changes. The low point of the family may have been reached in the last few years as affluence peaked; divorce rates rose along with affluence for years, and it should not be too surprising that these two trends paralleled each other. Affluence was hostile to the family; adversity will make it more valuable. In some cases this will mean that marriages will hold together out of economic necessity, marriages that in more affluent times would have broken up. Is this good or bad? It is of course impossible to generalize, but if the bleak economic prospects force individuals to change and compromise to sustain a marriage it could be a force for personal growth, in contrast to entering another marriage without a willingness to mold oneself to the needs of one's partner, a marriage that would also be unlikely to last. Certainly, making a marriage work is far more valuable for the children involved than serial marriages.

At any rate, it is reassuring to know that the family is there to help absorb whatever blows the future throws at us. The enjoyments of a strengthened family may be compensation for the tough adjustments elsewhere in society.

Going with the Grain of Nature

A good part of the family's continuing value is due to the hard work and the good heart that its members put into it. But for once, this effort is supported by instincts which, as with sex, work through our deepest being. To love a child is the easiest and purest form of love, free of the threat of rejection or the distortion of self-interest. A mother nursing her infant is a beautiful sight, perhaps the most beautiful sight of all—the new life, the abundant milk of the mother's breast, and her radiant joy in nurturing her child. The Catholic church had sure instincts when they made Mary and the Christ child a central image of the faithful.

The sexual urge is clear and strong, but so too are the urges to nurture the infant that the sexual urge leads to. The initial instincts are related to those of sex; a baby's cry causes uterine contractions in the mother and blood flows to her nipples and causes milk to flow even before she puts the baby to her breast. For mothers and their babies to have strong bonding, psychologists have found that it is essential that babies have extended physical contact with their mothers, prolonged eye contact, smiling, and soothing sounds, all of which breast feeding contributes to beautifully. With strong bonding, mothers feel closer to their children, have more concern for them, are more soothing, and give them more affection, all indicating both love for and enjoyment of their babies. After two years, babies with strong bonding smiled and laughed more, were healthier, and their mothers asked more questions and issued fewer commands to their babies. Not only is nurturing more important for us than any other species since we are born naked and helpless, but it is required for a longer period of time since our growth is slow. The generous instincts of nurture help assure this.

Unlike mothering, fathering does not seem to be instinctive. It is uncommon in primates, and is nonexistent in some human societies. But it is quite strong in other societies, and in studies where fathers are placed with their newborn infants, the same bonding occurs and fathers become more sensitive and affectionate with their children. There is now an increasing mass of data that demonstrates conclusively that children who do not receive enough love when young, physically and emotionally, are unable to love others when they grow up. Those who are deprived of love altogether become severely retarded or even die.

Nurturing must be one of the supreme examples of synergism, providing parents with joy and satisfaction and the child with the essentials needed for healthy development. It also suggests what may possibly be one of the most unfortunate parts of modern medical care: Who can tell how many of the difficulties young people are encountering today are due to quickly removing the child from the mother after birth, isolating it in a nursery, and discouraging breast feeding (which not only serves to bond mother and child together but also provides the child with essential nutrients and lifelong protections against disease)? We have made much progress on this recently, but there is still a good way to go to overcome the self-interest of the medical industry in professionalizing childbirth and making it expensive. Giving birth, after all, is a natural process that should not require the miracles of modern medicine. The nations with the lowest infant mortality rates, Holland especially but also England, are those that never got away from having normal births at home with the help of midwives, with the hospitals there to handle the few problem cases.

The family is a fully made garment, biologically, emotionally, and culturally, one that fits us well after being shaped by a long process of evolution. It is "gene deep," a magnificent gift if we have the wisdom, no, just the common sense, to accept it. But it requires that we be worthy of it, to forego our narcissism, our self-absorption, and our tendency to denigrate anything that is not new, different, or sophisticated.

The economy, however, will undoubtedly help us do this if it keeps on its current track.

The Resurgence of the Household Economy

Affluence permitted individuals to provide for themselves and to go their own ways; they didn't need the family. The generations were relieved of the difficult business of living and working together by wider job opportunities and improved retirement systems. The family was weakened as its economic functions were reduced, but it was by no means destroyed. It is ready to play a larger role as affluence turns into scarcity, as jobs for young people grow scarce, and as retirement programs no longer look as strong as they once did. The conditions that gave the family its key economic functions are returning, and returning quickly, and even if few people look forward to being dependent on the family once again after so many years of freedom and autonomy, the choices are either to learn how to work within the family or to find that the future is much more difficult than it need be.

In many families today, the older generations have a quite substantial share of the economic resources. Not only are they more likely to have a good job with the protections of seniority, but they also have homes either paid for or with a large equity, as well as savings in the bank. Young people are having a hard time even getting started—finding a job—let alone buying a home or starting a family. *It is a natural situation for parents to help their sons and daughters.* We have little experience in how to do this, and just as with so many other things in a declining economy, it is bound to be awkward. But the potential is there, and so is the precedent; this is the way it worked in the past. Parents can resist this, if they wish, and see the needs of their children as threatening the peace and prosperity of their retirement years. Or they can see it as an opportunity to be involved in the lives of their children, to work with them, help them, and enrich their own lives at the same time.

If the industrial economy has only a few jobs to offer young people coming out of schools and colleges, the only alternative for many of them will be to find some kind of unconventional work—some way to earn money outside the mainstream economy. There is no question that this will be much harder than stepping into a nine-to-five job with a paycheck at the end of the week, which most young people would prefer. But if such a job is not available and unemployment benefits have run out, there will be little choice; any income will be better than none. And some young people will inevitably opt out of the stiffening competition for the fewer well-paid jobs still available and think instead of something with less income but less pressure and more satisfactions.

Very often the ways to earn money that are identified will require capital to get started, and the older generation will be the natural source of financial help. This will not be a gift to young people and will not involve large amounts of money; the family assets will be considered far too important for that. The initial help may even be in the form of an activity in which parents can be partners of some sort. It may be only the skills parents pass on to young people, or the use of tools or a vehicle. It may be providing them with room and board or allowing the garage to be turned into a workspace. If things worked out satisfactorily, direct financial help may be provided—to rent a shop, purchase stock, or expand an operation.

It could be more than this too; it could be the opportunity for parents to try something they have long wanted to do but didn't feel young enough or energetic enough to try—starting up a part-time business, opening up a country store, or running a sheep ranch. The help of a younger generation—who will see the effort as being their inheritance if successful—could be the key element in a revitalized plan, encouraging the two generations to work together. Or it could be that this would be easier with an aunt and uncle rather than with parents, if growing up in this era has left relations strained with parents.

Grandparents also may be interested, perhaps in contributing assets to the enterprise to give it a better capital base to start from, or even in participating in the family venture. They could be a big help, leaving the younger generations with more time to get the nascent effort started and employing the skills that older people very often have—in repairing things, economizing, or working with animals—skills that younger people have had no reason to learn in this era of urban affluence. The abysmal lack of skills many of us have is no small obstacle to the emergence of the sustainable economy, and older people have many of the necessary skills. And there is little question that older people are happier when they are needed and have things to offer, especially in working with their children and grandchildren.

In some cases, this process may take the family back to where its roots are, back to family property or to places where relatives still live. A family network can be a real asset, helping to find opportunities, local materials, or part-time jobs. The extended family has more resources than the nuclear family, more contacts with which to fit people with needs, and to exchange services. It can help during a lean period with surplus vegetables from a garden, spare firewood, the use of an old rototiller, or even with shelter. This is one of the functions of the extended family, and it is bound to be useful again.

If it is correct that we will have more time and less money in the future, home production will be an increasing part of the household economy. This may be forced by the loss of a job by one spouse, which, if the fall in income is not to mean a substantial fall in living standards, will necessitate producing things at home to compensate for some of the lost income, such as expanding the size of a vegetable garden, baking bread, repairing the car, or doing maintenance on the house. It could also be voluntary, the decision that the cost of a second spouse working—in terms of child care, clothes, transportation, and income taxes—is so high that it takes too large a share of the income earned. This decision could be reached fairly soon, especially when the value of what could be produced at home is added into the cost of a job, such as cooking from scratch to avoid the high cost of prepared foods, sewing clothes, or the pleasure of being with children as they grow up rather than having to worry about how they are doing at school or a child-care center. The economic advantages of home production could improve rapidly if jobs grew scarcer, or wages were depressed by high unemployment.

The ultimate in home production is home production itself —building a house. This is a strenuous project and it is only possible under certain circumstances, but, if possible, it can be rewarding on an equally impressive scale, especially considering what it takes to buy a house these days. Building a house is a project the whole family can participate in, and for children it can provide experiences that benefit them for a lifetime. A number of people who have built their own home describe it as one of the high points of their lives. But it can be taxing on a family as well; the important point seems to be to keep the house modest in scale and not try to build it too fast.

As the sustainable economy begins to take shape, people's livelihood will increasingly be associated with the home—in stores with dwellings behind them or overhead, in workshops behind houses, or repair operations that work out of garages. These are familiar from the past and are still seen in places. They are enjoyable to patronize, but their key advantage is that they make full use of the family as an economic unit. A shop with a dwelling behind it, for example, can be open at all hours with one of the family members simply coming out to serve a customer who has been announced by a bell over the door. A simple sign can let customers know when the family will be away for the evening or on a vacation, and when the shop will be open again. The husband and the wife can share the work of watching over the store in the daytime, leaving both with time to do other things. And children can help too, with cleaning and even helping customers, gaining valuable experience in the adult world at the same time. A repair shop adjacent to a house makes it possible for a wife to answer calls and relay messages, and youngsters can help too, learning their father's skills as they do.

What all this means, in practical terms, is that a family-run operation will have lower expenses than a similar operation located in a shopping center, for example, primarily for labor but also for rent. It would take far less business to sustain a family in such a small-scale operation, and as it becomes more expensive to drive to a shopping center, business at neighborhood shops will improve. Granted, the hourly wage of family members may be quite modest, but it can be pleasurable work, especially as neighborhoods become more sociable places. The work will avoid the necessity of commuting, will permit a good deal of flexibility, and should avoid the pressures of a large office or the monotony of the assembly line. It will mean balanced roles for men and women in a cooperative family enterprise, and good experiences for children growing up. But most importantly, it will be strengthened by cooperation within the family enterprise rather than weakened by individuals following different paths in the mainstream economy. It will mean that families will pull together rather than pull apart.

A Return to Large Families?

If the past is a guide, the strengthening of the family may bring with it a tendency toward larger families. The pleasures of children and their contributions to family life are great—the sound of their young voices, their innocence, their delight in everything, their growth through the stages of life, and the sons-in-law or daughters-in-law they eventually marry.

The geriatric society toward which we are heading, one dominated by older people and with few children, pales in comparison to a society full of young people. Still, any trend toward larger families must be resisted. *Population control is intrinsically a part of a sustainable way of life.*

It is true, as certain "optimists" never tire of saying, that we could support a larger population than today, even if industrial resources grew scarce. We have roughly one-fourth the population of China and the same amount of land. On this basis, we could enjoy the luxury of large families for quite a while. But this leaves several huge issues: Do we want to live the way the Chinese do? Could the productivity of the environment be sustained under such intense use without the roughly four thousand years of experience the Chinese have had? And when the point is reached when population growth must be stopped, is there any evidence that this can be accomplished before life deteriorates under the effect of too many people? Even in China, where the tradition of obedience to authority is far higher than here and where the government is offering incentives to have *one child* per family, population growth is still expected to continue for a good many years and bring the population to 1.2 billion people by the year 2000.

In contrast, we are now in a situation where public concern about overpopulation is high and birth rates are low, and it is essential that we preserve these values and make small families a part of the cultural heritage we hand on to our children. *Low birth rates could well be one of our main gifts to the future.* If lost, and large families were allowed to return, the trend would undoubtedly be as difficult for us to reverse as it is proving to be in less developed countries today.

The reasons for smaller families today range all across the spectrum. Many people are concerned about overpopulation or feel they can contribute more to the well-being of society without children. Financial factors are forcing couples to postpone having children or to have fewer children. When couples work, they often get used to their high combined incomes and are simply unwilling to reduce their affluence and personal freedom to have children. And raising children is more demanding today than it was in the past, more expensive and less satisfying in several important ways. All of these are good reasons for couples not to have children, which is just as it should be. There are already too many children growing up without the love and attention they need to grow into healthy human beings. If there is any question about a couple's willingness to provide these to a child, they are correct in not having children. The main problem today is the people who are having children without this commitment.

Abortion is a major factor in controlling unwanted pregnancies worldwide. It is repulsive to almost everyone, but it has been used since time immemorial. The Bible nowhere speaks against it, and it was not until the nineteenth century that a social movement against it began. Those who seek to ban it —an understandable impulse—must ask themselves if they are willing to take the responsibility for the unwanted children that would result. The greatest tragedy today, both for the child and society, is for a child to grow up unloved and unwanted. And who can say that this does not happen all too commonly?

Birth rates are down now for a number of reasons, but the sustainable economy will remove a good many of these reasons. And given the pleasures of children and the increased role of the family, it is quite likely that there will be a tendency for family size to increase. Yet at some stage a growing population would be forced to a halt anyway in any number of disagreeable ways, and then we would be forced back to small family size under much less satisfactory circumstances.

Consider all the advantages, both economic and environmental, of maintaining a two-child family and a stable population. With an average of two children, it will not be necessary to be continually building more homes, extending utilities and roads, building new schools, fire stations, police departments, and libraries, and covering up needed land to do so. Rather, it will be possible to spend public funds to *improve* what we already have, to improve schools, embellish parks and public spaces, and buy more books for libraries rather than simply trying to keep up with new needs. Young people will be able to occupy jobs vacated by older people, so that society will not have to be frantically trying to generate new jobs all the time. All this would mean more leisure and a community that is improving in quality, rather than one that is struggling to find new jobs for a large number of young people and being forced to use more resources to do so.

To keep population well below the carrying capacity of the environment also means there will be less stress on the environment. It is not only destructive to plow steep slopes that are vulnerable to erosion, to denude hills of trees, and to overgraze hillsides, but it also takes a great deal of effort and produces a thin livelihood as well. It means being forced to take a small crop off of an eroded field on a hillside, cutting young trees for wood, or slaughtering thin and scrawny animals with little meat on them. And the next year may be worse as resources will have been further depleted and the productivity of the land will have been reduced. *The good life is achieved with a population well below the carrying capacity of the environment*, and this is the point we are at today —or could be as we are slowly forced away from the heavy consumption of the industrial era. It is in living well below the limits that the sustainable economy gains its ease, and the security of knowing that the environment is not being threatened by overexploitation. It is a luxury that few nations can enjoy, one that is imperative to hold on to if it is to be part of the heritage we pass on to future generations.

But this brings us back to the problem of the double bind. If some families or groups control their numbers, they run the risk of being swamped by those who do not. Hardin's answer, of mutual coercion mutually agreed upon, is the only possible answer, but to carry it out requires an effective community, one that is capable of protecting itself in whatever ways necessary, including guarding against overpopulation. We do not have that kind of a community today and to establish it will be much more difficult than is generally realized. It will be far harder than to revitalize the family, which never really ceased being at the center of people's lives. But community is just as important, and it provides many of the same kinds of pleasures of belonging and mutual support.

8

Community, the Harder Step

In a paper titled "Counterintuitive Behavior of Social Systems," Jay Forrester of the Massachusetts Institute of Technology posed a problem for individuals trying to improve their community. Forrester argued that people will keep moving from one place to another until every place is equally unattractive, at which time movement will cease since people cannot better themselves by moving. In other words, anything a community does to improve itself, whether to improve amenities, provide jobs, or reduce the cost of living, is self-defeating since it will only attract other people until this relative attractiveness no longer exists. If a community is trying to protect itself from being swamped by an inflow of people, the proper thing to do would be to make the community unattractive in order to discourage people from coming.

That such irrational behavior contains an element of logic is a reflection of how problematic community is in this country. On the surface, the idea of community is warmly supported almost everywhere, but on a more fundamental level, there are pervasive problems with community, and even hostility to it in a number of instances. *It is not that we dislike community, it is just that we value our individual freedoms more.* We are attracted to neighborliness and social interaction, but do not like it when it turns out that community also means restrictions on our freedom for the larger good of the community. *But without the willingness to restrain oneself for a common good, there is no effective community.* This is the tragedy of the commons again. Without community, there is no method of identifying what the common good is and working to preserve and enhance it. Obviously, as the term is used here, community means much more than trying to maintain the property values of a neighborhood or providing adequate police protection; these are private demands made on local government. Community here means a primary context for people's lives, of people working together to provide things in common that they cannot provide in any other way.

Mobility and Freedom

Our constitutional protections cover a number of freedoms, including the freedom to live where we want to. We all value this freedom highly; it is one that has shaped the American character in many positive ways, contributing to the dynamism and openness of our society. But this freedom also contains a dilemma: It makes it possible for individuals to exploit an environment or a community and move on. Any community that managed to make itself safe and comfortable would attract people from communities that had been allowed to become ugly and dangerous. The freedom to move is an incentive for individuals to be irresponsible—to vote for low taxes, to skimp on public services, to cut corners on maintaining streets and public buildings, or to exploit the environment for economic gain—and then, before the results begin to show too obviously, to sell their property and move on. And the community that has been responsible will be a natural place to move to, an ideal opportunity for the irresponsible to repeat the process of capitalizing on other people's responsibility.

The boom-and-bust pattern so common in American history is a natural expression of our freedom to move. Settlers skimmed off the fertility of farm lands, cut the best forests, and took the high-grade minerals and headed farther west, leaving abandoned towns and depressed regions. Even during this century we deserted industrial regions for sunnier, fresher areas, and until recently we left our central cities to those people who could afford nothing better. This pattern is still going on; we exploit our land, natural resources, new technologies, and consumer gimmicks for all they are worth, and then look elsewhere for fields that are still green. These are freedoms our Constitution protects.

And we have enjoyed these freedoms; there are real pleasures in these irresponsibilities. If our history has been reckless in the way it treated the land, it has also been boisterous and enthusiastic, full of excitement and opportunity. But we can be entirely certain that our irresponsibility will come back to haunt us some day; at some point there will not be any green fields left; every place will be equally unattractive and equally exploited—which is the way many areas are already. The end of the frontier, whether in land, resources, economic growth, or technological advance, means an end to the openness that we value so much in American life. This fear of closure is behind the enthusiasm for space colonization, which would bring back the joyful freedoms of the frontier. But it would take huge amounts of energy to push many space vehicles away from the earth's gravitational force, energy which we do not have, and we will either replace the joys of irresponsibility with the joys of community—of which there are many—or we will find our world closing in on us in many unwanted ways.

Our freedoms and the absence of effective community has made a good part of this country into a commons, and like all commons, there are many ready to exploit it, but few who are willing to care for it. But Hardin's solution—of "mutual coercion, mutually agreed upon"—would be unconstitutional in a number of ways. Translated into mobility, for example, it would force Americans to stay where they are. This may not appeal to us and is certainly not feasible today, but consider how it would change our behavior. There would be incentive for people to get to work and make their community a good one since they would have to live with it the rest of their lives. There would be a clear logic to practice careful husbandry of the land on which the material well-being of present and future generations rested; exploiting the environment to its utmost for momentary gain would, in this context, be irrational. People would build houses that lasted hundreds of years, as they did in medieval times, rather than flimsy structures to be bought and sold for speculation.

To be able to offer incentives such as these is what gives community its power. And when this power is taken away, as it is under the American legal system, local government becomes little more than an institution for dispensing services mandated by higher levels of government. The national government is the only one to which we give an oath of allegiance, the only entity of which we are clearly a member, but it is too large, too remote, and too bureaucratic to function as a community.

Is Individual Freedom Antagonistic to Community?

As it stands now, the answer to this question must be yes. We see community as interfering with our freedom to do what we want, and freedom has the higher value to us. To restrain community is at times beneficial—when community means white people systematically holding down black people or union solidarity means allowing only members' sons to join. But in other cases, our constitutional protections facilitate the exploitation that community traditionally controlled since these protections must be applied indiscriminately. They not only protect the rights of black children to go to white schools, but they also protect the rights of businessmen to evict old people from apartments to turn them into condominiums, to employ advertising that makes people dissatisfied with what they have or anxious about their personal hygiene, and to build subdivisions on land planned for a park if public funds to buy the land cannot be raised quickly enough. An individual can own pornography shops in the inner city and still be a respected resident of a fine neighborhood. And if a community tried to resist these things it would be declared unconstitutional, in violation of individual civil liberties, or in restraint of trade. If a community tried to require reciprocity, establish mutual obligations, or require landowners to preserve the productivity of their land, this too would be declared unconstitutional. And to establish membership in a community would be deemed discriminatory.

Our political process, too, illustrates how little enthusiasm we have for community. All of us have been more than willing to let the government take responsibilities we wanted to shed, and to let an anonymous bureaucracy handle the unpleasant tasks of caring for the poor, the elderly, the mentally ill, the criminals, and the unwanted children so that we could be free to do things more to our liking. If we see someone beside a car broken down on the road, a drunk on the sidewalk, or an old lady sleeping on a park bench at night, we can pass by with a clear conscience, if we choose, because there are people hired with our tax dollars to take care of such things. Individuals in a community used to feel responsibility for such people, but now we have impersonal institutions to take care of them, institutions which remove us from much of the nitty-gritty of life, rather like the sanitized meat under plastic wrappers in the supermarket that protects us from the impression that a living animal has been killed to get it there. Schoolchildren take trips to old people's homes and mental institutions to learn about things that in the past were a part of everyone's life. These institutions make everything in our society look neat and tidy (or they are supposed to), leaving the unsavory parts of life out of sight, unnaturally so, rather like the cancer-causing pollutants unseen in our water and air. If things go poorly in the schools, the courts, or the cancer wards, we can stand back and blame those we have hired to do our tough jobs for us.

Still, we yearn for community. We sense that we are missing something important: the willingness of people to help one another, the feelings of rootedness in a place, the feelings of belonging, of safety, of continuity.

Yet we are torn; we like the anonymity of cities, for example, and the freedom to do what we want without someone looking over our shoulder reprimanding us for our actions or reminding us of our obligations. The trouble is that the exploiters, from the mugger up to the one in the gray flannel suit, also appreciate this anonymity; they capitalize on it to take from others in all manner of ways. We would like to have the benefits of community, but are unwilling to pay the price. We are not willing to temper some basic American freedoms,

freedoms that have shaped our national character and made this country great, especially not for something as questionable and potentially oppressive as community. The extraordinary success of the United States in terms of political continuity and economic progress are more than enough to support the conclusion that we are unlikely to see any political or constitutional changes that might make community easier —at least not while there are pleasures still left in our irresponsibilities.

In lieu of community, we have many voluntary associations, and their services and contributions have often been extraordinary. Some require major commitments for membership and come to serve many of the functions of community, especially religious groups. But most associations make light demands on their members and are rather fluid and superficial. Individuals float in and out, looking for something that satisfies their need to belong. But commitment is difficult to sustain, and there are frustrations in trying to find individuals willing to take responsibility for the ongoing needs of the organization. Those who do the work often feel taken advantage of by others; they begin to feel like fools when others are reluctant to carry their share of the responsibility of keeping an organization going. The organization rarely can be counted on; it cannot gain the strength and confidence that comes from overcoming adversity when it is so easy for people to leave. Few voluntary associations provide the continuity and the comprehensive framework of human affinities that people are looking for. We are attracted by solidarity, but repelled by its demands.

In traditional communities, membership is exceedingly important. It usually stems from birth, from being born into a neighborhood or a village, into an economic unit such as a guild or a caste, or into a religious community. The community is what defines one's world and thus is the basis of one's self-image. Membership is prized as life itself. We see this time and again throughout history, in Italian city-states, in primitive hunting and gathering societies, in the charter towns and manors of Europe, and in African tribal societies. To be ostracized is the worst possible punishment; in English medieval terminology, to be an "outlaw" was to be placed outside the law of the community one was born into. Once ostracized in this way, it was very difficult to gain admittance to another community since such an outsider was assumed to be a dangerous person: why would they be outside a community unless they were thrown out? In many languages, the word for *stranger* is the same as the word for *enemy*. This suspicion of outsiders is noticeable even in the United States —in New England, for example—where it is necessary to prove oneself by long years of good service before full membership in the community is earned. In such a world oaths are important, in contrast to our society where one of the few remaining oaths, for marriage, is broken in about half of the instances. This would be unthinkable in traditional society, suggesting an unacceptable lack of loyalty and steadfastness.

As things stand now, community and freedom do seem antagonistic in this country. But this is a highly unusual conflict; in most cultures, *individual freedom can only be understood within the firm structure of a community, which gives a context and significance to an individual's life.* The function of community in traditional societies is similar to the function of the family and roles; it defines the world people live in, defines the rules of the game of life, in much the way that the economy and politics define our world. The fact that traditional societies have all sorts of eccentrics and characters even though they impose rigid boundaries on behavior suggests that, within these boundaries, there is a wide area where individuals have the freedom, and the security, to be themselves. In our society, by contrast, conformity can be seen as stemming from the needs of individuals to gain acceptance in informal groups, and the way to do that is to try to be as much like the people in that group as possible. *Freedom, rather than being the liberating force for individuals it is commonly made out to be, could well be an intimidating, threatening force instead.*

It is unfortunate that Americans have had so little experience with community, so little chance to know how satisfying it can be. Sometimes it is felt under wartime conditions, when soldiers must depend on others, or in times of adversity, such as the Depression. But for the most part, we think of it in terms of restraint, a community trying to keep us from doing things we want to do. We usually want to make our own way, to earn our own glory, rather than to express ourselves through a community. America has not always been so obsessed with individualism, but neither is it possible to say that the history of community in this country offers a great deal of encouragement either.

American Experience with Community

In the seventeenth and eighteenth centuries, Europe was in the midst of tumultuous change. The old order—the landed aristocracy and the church—was struggling with the rising commercial classes for ascendency, a struggle that was tearing apart the traditional village society, all made more bitter by religious conflict. It was a corrupt time, and the attractions of America for land as well as freedom were great indeed.

The first settlers to make the long and dangerous journey to this remote and wild continent had to be highly motivated, and this initially came from religious persecution in Europe. And as is often the case, once those who had been oppressed gained their release, they turned and oppressed others. But the Puritans were soon overwhelmed by other newcomers, and the colonial era was a period of quite satisfactory community; even the landscape assumed the shape of rural England with its villages, towns, fields, and woods. The self-governing New England town meetings are an important part of our history. With transportation limited, each village and town had to be responsible for much of its own needs. This economic activity—the shoemaker, the carpenter, the blacksmith, the wheelwright—gave these settlements a bustling activity they lost in the nineteenth century when the railroads brought in factory-made goods and towns shriveled to a handful of stores, a bank, and a train depot.

The nineteenth century was a period of fundamental change all through our society as immigrants poured in from foreign countries, factories destroyed time-honored trades and skills, and cities grew to a size people never dreamed possible. The industrial era was coming into its own, and this was profoundly disturbing to many. This was the century of the great religious revivals and the return to the Puritan values of the Victorian period; both can be seen as efforts to reestablish ways that were being threatened by modern changes.

It was also the century of the utopian communities that came to form such a conspicuous strain in our history. In all, some ninety-one communities were formed during the nineteenth century, reflecting all the social movements of the time: primitive Christianity, pacificism, women's rights, communism, socialism, free love, celibacy, temperance, and anarchism. In all this diversity, however, there was a common thread—the quest for community and the harmony, order, peace, and brotherhood so conspicuously absent in the early industrial era. Some communities were formed by intellectuals (such as Brook Farm, which attracted Nathaniel Hawthorne) and some were organized by simple folk taken with religious zeal, such as Ann Lee Stanley, one of eight children born to a poor blacksmith in Manchester, England, who brought her small band of followers to this country to form the largest and longest lasting group, the Shakers.

These communities are a fascinating part of our history, but they cannot be considered to have been successful. Fewer than twelve lasted for more than sixteen years, and the overwhelming majority lasted less than four years. One of the most ambitious efforts, Robert Owens's New Harmony, was dissolved after two years. Instead of peace and brotherhood, the communities experienced disagreement, bitterness, and, ultimately, failure. They were plagued by all the problems that make human relationships difficult: communism was unable to overcome the tendency toward private accumulation; neither celibacy nor free love were able to solve the age-old problems associated with the power of the sexual drive; the family continued to compete with the community for primary loyalty and undermined the communal order; initial religious enthusiasms were difficult to maintain in an increasingly secular society. Several groups survived as commercial ventures after the communities broke down, most notably Amana and Oneida, and the Shakers threw themselves increasingly into economic activities as the community itself began to weaken. The word *utopia* comes from a Latin word meaning *nowhere*, a place that does not exist, suggesting that it is contrary to human nature. The utopian community movement in this country confirms such a definition.

The second period of interest in communities, the commune movement of the 1960s, had an even shorter history. The logic seemed good enough—people taking advantage of the affluence of this society to live simply and close to nature, working only enough to provide for modest needs, and enjoying each other and the environment. But this was too good to be true; the nuts and bolts of what it takes to make a community work were not there. It was assumed that everyone could "do their own thing" and still get along fine—the common American hope that community does not have to include restraint. But conflicts soon led to failure; the only ones that survived for any length of time were those that adopted a religious structure. An excellent book dealing with the difficulties and the benefits of making a commune work is Benjamin Zablocki's *The Joyful Community*. It is not an easy task. The fact that there are very few examples of communal societies in the world, other than hunters and gatherers, suggests that they are hard to sustain.

At least we can say that we learned something from these experiments with intentional communities. We learned what does not work—communities that stray too far from the traditional pattern. There is more to learn from the successful communities in this country, which have very different characteristics.

Ethnic communities provide a good example. They had their origins in the needs of new immigrants to get their feet on the ground in a strange country, to learn the language and new ways of doing things. Often the immigrants needed loans, help finding a place to live, and a job. The integrating force was the common heritage of "the old country," the language, the customs, the foods, and the feelings of being dependent on one another. This function weakened as the younger generations become more at home in American society, but many ethnic communities survive because they continue to provide important services to their members. One of the most notable ones today is protection against crime. Ethnic communities generally are safe because people know each other; if a stranger is seen on the streets, people keep an eye on him from the sidewalks, the front porches, and the shops; a thief or a mugger is not able to melt into a faceless crowd as he can in other parts of the city. There is an obligation to help people in such a community, people who are their friends. Crime in general is closely related to the strength of a community; it is in the absence of community that a person can scream for help with none forthcoming. Community, if it means anything, means being involved, which is just the opposite of wanting to go about one's own business without being disturbed.

The Amish provide the most complete example of a community in the United States, one that has kept the influence of outside ways to the minimum possible. Not only have the Amish survived as a community, but they have done so under the most extraordinary circumstances—as small farmers using horses and buggies in an era of large mechanized farms. Moreover, they are successful enough that they are still able to buy farms for their sons out of their earnings from farming.

The success of the Amish community comes in large part from the tenacity with which they have held to their traditional ways. The Amish are on the left wing of the Protestant Reformation—they believe in individual interpretation of the Bible, which led them to believe in adult baptism since a child could not be expected to make a rational decision to accept the faith. To be Anabaptists seems reasonable enough today, but in the upheavals of sixteenth- and seventeenth-century Europe, it was deemed heretical by the Lutheran authorities. The result was persecution in which virtually all of the educated Amish leadership was put to death. The remaining Amish fell back on their traditions as the main defense against the outside world. Persecution in Europe welded the Amish into a strong community, strong enough to preserve their way of life after immigrating to America in the eighteenth century. The Amish, who were progressive for centuries in both religion and agriculture, are now felt to be one of the best sources of insight into peasant farming life in sixteenth-century Germany.

Like most peasant communities, the Amish are primarily concerned with sustaining a way of life. They pay taxes but do not accept government services. They will not hold office, bear arms, or use force. Outside the community, the Amish are crafty bargainers, while inside the community exchange replaces money in most cases. The cost of an extended illness is made up by the community, and a barn that burns down is rebuilt communally. Each church district is small, based on the distances buggies can travel to church services, and each has its own church officers, who are chosen by lot to avoid the pride that would accompany election.

The Bible is the source of authority to the Amish, but interpreting it for instruction is not easy, given the modern world they live in, and consequently disputes have caused the Amish to split into several different orders. The Amish have reached different decisions on such matters as how extensively machinery should be used or how rigidly dress codes should be enforced. But they still share a wide heritage. Farming is the preferred occupation because the first chapter of the Bible directs mankind to replenish the earth and have dominance over animals and the land. 2 Corinthians says "Be ye not unequally yoked to unbelievers," which the Amish interpret to mean not being tied to electrical and telephone lines. And since the Bible speaks of draft animals but not tractors, the Amish do not use tractors. Because pride is a sin much to be guarded against, the Amish prescribe the type of clothing to be worn and how the hair is to be cut. And as with other peasant communities, ostracism is the worst punishment. It is rare, however, as is the intermediate form of *meidung*, or shunning, in which no one will speak to a person who refuses to repent a sin.

The Amish, like all peasants, are known for their durability, for bending just enough to preserve their way of life without losing its valued qualities. Most Amish use chemical fertilizers, have specialists analyze their soil and feed requirements, and use refrigeration units and milking machines in order to meet government health requirements. In Pennsylvania, Amish farmers use half the fossil fuels to produce just as much milk per acre as their non-Amish neighbors, and in their homes they use only 10 percent as much fossil fuel energy as their neighbors. A good case can be made that the simple Amish technology is more practical than the sophisticated solar technologies that are currently being promoted as the wave of the future. But the key advantage the Amish have is their community. It preserves a trusted and valued way of life and assures its members of mutual aid and cooperation, all within the framework of religious beliefs that have sustained the Amish for almost three hundred years.

Community and the Sustainable Economy

Community will undoubtedly be an essential element of the sustainable economy. But the barriers to community—political, legal, and those in the American character—are each very substantial. How will it be possible to establish community against such odds?

The history of community in this country tells us several things. One is that intentional communities, and especially communes, are very difficult to sustain. The grand visions are too remote and unattainable and are usually destroyed by the small day-to-day problems. Successful communities are far more likely to be based on the needs of individuals, families, and groups, with the community simply evolving out of the struggle to make life good. Successful communities are usually associated with a specific place—a neighborhood, a town, a valley. They are usually small so that people can deal with each other on a face-to-face basis rather than in a legalistic or bureaucratic way. And membership serves to identify those who are part of the moral community—those with shared obligations—and those who are not. But most importantly, the community must provide something that individuals cannot provide on their own.

Clearly, all these conditions would be difficult to meet, and we may assume that some communities are possible without all of them, especially as economic conditions grow tougher. But it is still hard to anticipate how community will find expression in the future. The possibilities are wide, but where the conditions will be most fertile is difficult to say. The leadership of a single individual could well be the critical variable.

Of the conditions that support community, a number are easier to establish in rural areas. The number of people is smaller; they have a clearer common interest to protect than in a large, economically diverse urban area; their interests are more clearly related to the productivity of the local environment; and there are probably fewer differences in values held. Social selection is also likely to be at work here too; people oriented toward community will gravitate toward rural areas compared to those who appreciate the city's anonymity, higher incomes, and wider range of activities.

The prospects for community will also increase with geographic isolation. To be distant from other towns and cities will mean that the cost of bringing in goods will be higher, giving locally produced goods a cost advantage. People will be less reluctant to share tools when rental shops are miles away and to exchange services when craftsmen are not as close as the Yellow Pages of the phone book. Isolation will mean that people will look to the community for social activities and will be more likely to know each other than in less isolated places. This social community is important, for it will form the basis for common action when more serious problems arise.

A slowing economy will mean that jobs and money become scarce, and a community could face gradual impoverishment unless it can reduce the flow of money out of the community. The initial reaction will be to find new products to export, but this will be difficult in a depressed economy. The alternative will be to reduce imports by using locally produced goods, keeping money circulating within the community rather than losing it to the outside. However, local production is bound to be less efficient, and even avoiding the cost of transportation and other overhead expenses, local goods, in many cases, will be more expensive. The community's natural tendency will be to discriminate against imported goods, something that will be facilitated by the face-to-face contact of an open-air market and exchange between people who are not only buyers and sellers but neighbors and friends.

Such discrimination against outside goods will surely generate a hostile response by suppliers of these goods. But to the degree that local production becomes important to the livelihood of the community, the discrimination is likely to continue. It could lead to legal action—to court challenges of community activities that are in restraint of free trade. Regulatory agencies are also likely to become a problem, since local activities are bound to take shortcuts around regulations appropriate for the mainstream economy but not for an isolated community. Thus the requirement that cattle be shipped to distant slaughterhouses to be federally inspected and graded can be avoided, as can the stringent sanitary requirements for large modern dairies, the rigid safety requirements for large saw mills, and the expensive requirements of building codes that were designed to make sure builders of huge housing projects do not cut corners. It is the outside industries that are hurt that will press for the enforcement of such regulations, but the community will be able to evade many of these efforts simply by keeping their activities quiet, by ceasing prohibited activities only temporarily, starting them up elsewhere, or in the case of building codes, by simply having everyone ignore unnecessary ones when building their own houses. The absence of a local government would be an advantage since there would be no formal body for regulatory agencies to challenge. A Saturday market could evolve into an informal town meeting for the discussion of problems and strategies. Such activity is what has made public markets vital in the past, playing important roles in the economic, political, and social life of the community.

There may also be attempts by a major employer within a community to pay low wages in response to high unemployment in the national economy. Again, the community can thwart this if its members can act in concert. They could, for example, boycott the employer and make things uncomfortable for him in town. If the employer brings in other workers, the town could refuse to provide them services. There is a danger here, however, that the community may not want to accept the economic conditions under which the employer is working, conditions that may require falling wages. The community will have to consider its actions carefully here; driving an employer out of business will not help anybody, just as evading a necessary public health regulation could be disastrous.

The same thing is true in the way wealth is treated. The ideal is to exercise enough pressure on people with wealth to cause them to contribute generously to the public good—and thus gain honor and respect—but not to alienate potential benefactors with heavy-handed pressures. We may find this difficult to achieve in this country because people do not like to do things under pressure, especially to give things away. Still, it is no fun to be rich and alone in an isolated community—another example of how isolation is an advantage in facilitating community.

If commercial agriculture grew unprofitable, a large landowner's only alternative may be to allow local people to use his land under various possible arrangements. This would give the landowner some return, give people access to land who could not afford to buy it, and shift production toward goods for local consumption.

As the evolution of community proceeds, an increasing consciousness of the boundaries of the community will appear. If outsiders such as government agents, suppliers, and absentee landowners work against the community, a general suspicion of all outsiders may grow. The court system too may come to be considered as working against the interests of the community if it is used by outsiders to overcome the community's efforts to protect itself or if lawyers' fees and court costs are too high or the proceedings too slow. All of this will serve to reinforce the community's tendency to try to do everything they possibly can themselves. They will try to solve problems locally, perhaps by hearing disputes in the public market or accepting the decision of an arbitrator or a group of respected members of the community. Parents will be charged with constraining unruly young people rather than calling the police. This is not to supercede the authority of government agencies or the courts, but just to avoid using them if at all possible or to accomplish the same function in ways that are more satisfactory or quicker and less expensive to the people involved.

Under these circumstances, taxes will increasingly be seen as an economic drain on the community, as money that goes out of the community and, when it does come back, often returns in the form of unneeded services or harassment by government bureaucrats. The tendency will be for people to try to reduce the taxes paid. An ideal income will be seen as just below the point where federal income taxes must be paid. Sales taxes are hard to collect from open-air markets, barter, and informal exchanges. Schemes may even be hatched to drive down property values artificially so as to reduce property taxes. None of these things are likely to make the community popular with outsiders, but they will strengthen the identity of the community and its members.

Urban areas will not experience such clear manifestations of community, but economic adversity will encourage many of the same elements. As more of life is lived within neighborhoods, local meeting places will form, and from them will come ideas of how to help neighborhood businesses and craftsmen, how to provide work for young people, and how to avoid high-priced commodities and governmental regulations. Ways to exchange goods and services on an ever smaller basis will appear, which will encourage home production. Social and recreational activities will increasingly evolve around local meeting places—parks, schools, churches, cafés and night spots—rather than large commercial entertainments elsewhere. With more people knowing each other, crime will be reduced, and the community will be more able to defend itself against those who are perceived as working against the community's interests.

This is community. It is not peaceful and idyllic; it throbs with life—work, talk, dispute, setbacks, success. It is not free from conflict, but the conflict is increasingly with outsiders, which gives the community its unity and identity. To the degree that individuals see their own interests as synonymous with the community's, the basic requirement for community exists—its ability to provide services individuals cannot provide on their own. This feeling of working together for the common good is an important part of the good life. It is not entirely a safe process; community, just like anything else, can be carried too far and become oppressive. But still, community is essential if self-seeking individuals are to be encouraged to be responsible members of a society.

Ideally, the reemergence of community would be a process of voluntary grouping into many different communities reflecting different qualities—different environments, economic activities, religious beliefs. philosophical values, ethnic backgrounds. Individuals could choose the community they felt best in—including the alternative of noncommunity, most likely in certain parts of large cities. But this is probably too much to hope for; the actual process is likely to be much more of a rough-and-ready affair as we struggle to learn how to work together as a part of a community rather than as individuals in a fluid, large-scale society. The greatest problem is likely to be that too many individuals will refuse to give up their right to look at society opportunistically, or that community will not be strong enough to defend itself against these opportunists. Community, even if far from perfect, is still the best way to encourage social responsibility, and to give social relations some of the same trust and loyalty found in families and among friends.

9

The Human Landscape: The Surest Gift from the Past

This chapter offers a respite from the ambiguous and difficult cultural questions we have been dealing with in the last few chapters. Here we will look at some of the *physical* achievements of the past we can still *see* (and even live in if we are fortunate): cities that are human in scale and full of life; agreeable towns and villages; comfortable houses built with local materials and simple tools; and land worked in gentle and sustainable ways, landscapes that are still among the most desirable places to live. This subject had to wait until this point in the book because the traditional landscape is very much a reflection of a community and its ideals, just as our man-made environment reflects the aspirations of individuals and private businesses.

This is not to say that modern homes are not comfortable or that skyscraping corporate headquarters are not splendid achievements; they are. But there is also a broad consensus that our cities—the places where most of us live—are not working well. We have lavish private environments—fine homes, country clubs, and shopping centers—but overall, our cities, unfriendly and expensive, are places that many people are trying to get away from; they are often defaced with advertising and litter, and plagued with crime.

People will evaluate the merits of modern and traditional places according to their own tastes, but there is no question about the basic issue: *The old designs can be sustained with little use of energy; the modern ones cannot.* Even those who feel very comfortable with modern cities will appreciate the economy of older ways as cities become more of a strain on our pocketbooks because of the energy they require for their metabolism.

Because others have done the design work for us here, and done it well—often through hundreds and even thousands of years of experimentation—we are the beneficiaries of a great gift from the past. We can select the forms that we find most congenial and adapt them to our needs. We can add elements our ancestors did not have—good insulation and glass for light, warmth, and passive solar heating; electricity for lighting and refrigeration; and modern electronics for communications. But these modern advances cannot be the core of the matter. Look at what we have built with our remarkable tools and building materials plus huge amounts of money. Our cities are painful reminders to us that power and affluence do not assure a commodious way of life, and if rural areas are a bit better off, it is only because they have seen less "development" in recent decades. No, the designs of the past are more valuable than what we have been able to add, designs that could turn a wide array of indigenous materials into attractive yet affordable dwellings, into towns and cities that permitted not only an easy sociability but the earning of livelihoods as well, and all of it based on a sustainable use of the environment. These are substantial aesthetic achievements as well, all the more so because they are art for life. Such designs are not the towering achievements of Western civilization that are honored in museums or university art courses or were commissioned for wealthy patrons. They are, instead, the everyday achievements of ordinary people building and rebuilding over a long period of time, adding to what went before them, adding to the richness and fullness of human experience while still maintaining the productivity of the environment.

But even these, the surest gifts from the past, will not be easy for us to use. There are two basic difficulties. One is the world we have built for ourselves today, which so clearly reflects our abundance—sprawling cities, tall office towers, and huge industrial plants, all dependent on complex transportation networks. These are impressive achievements, but they depend heavily on energy to function. As energy grows scarcer and more expensive, they will become progressively less useful; even modifying them to preserve their usefulness will be awkward. The second problem is in our minds; we are likely to resist living closer to each other as people did in the past—in smaller houses, clustered together to facilitate interaction. Our man-made world reflects our preoccupation with privacy and our antipathy toward community, feelings which are inappropriate for a future that demands more cooperation and more use of human muscles. This will change, but not until the community begins to play a more important role in our lives.

Because of the difficulties we start with, it is almost impossible to foresee how we will use the design wisdom of the past. For now, it is easier—and more enjoyable—to simply look at these achievements to gain a feeling for how they worked and their logic for more frugal times. The examples that follow are from Europe, where most of our roots were before being transplanted to frontier soils. In one sense, the examples given are ideal forms; they are not used as they were by the people who built them. But the frontier is going too, and scarcity will give the traditional forms renewed life. For anyone who wants to build for the centuries, these are the ideas to start with. *They are presented in the belief that the kind of inspired craftsmen who built them in the past still exist in our midst today, and will resume the process of building and rebuilding that was interrupted by the industrial era.*

A Village

The village is often said to be the world in a microcosm. The one on the banks of the Loire River in France shown in the photograph on page 164 illustrates what is meant by this. There are three centers of interest in the village world: the land on which the livelihood of the village rests; the houses of the families that comprise the basic social unit in the community; and the village center with its church, a symbol of its ethical integration, and the small market square in front of it that provides for its functional integration—spaces for social gathering and exchange.

The houses that line the streets are strategically located, with the social world to the front and the natural world to the rear. On one side is the street, with children playing, people walking past, and a few shops, before leading away to the central square. On the other side are the kitchen gardens, flowers and fruit trees, and a few barns for the local cows before leading away to the fields and woods. It is "strip development," but in a satisfying way, beautifully balanced be-

A village on the banks of the Loire River in France. (*Photo credit: Charles E. Rotkin, Photography for Industry.*)

tween the needs of sociability on the street side of the houses and nature and privacy on the garden side.

In traditional societies, homes are very rarely the focus of social life. They are almost always small in size, leaving social life to go on elsewhere, on the sidewalks, in the shops, the public squares, and, in winter, around a blazing fire in inns, pubs, or cafés. The home, in contrast, is part of the private world of the family, large enough for it to gather together but not for social gatherings or to provide beds for guests.

The smallness of the houses has a number of advantages that still hold today. It made them inexpensive since less land, materials, and construction work was needed to build them. The small volume of space enclosed meant they were easier to furnish and to heat. They had an intimacy that is basic to close family relationships. They were built by local craftsmen in traditional styles, which not only avoided the expense of an architect but also circumvented planning commission hearings and building permits, since community norms were well established by custom. Building styles reflected a long evolution, incorporating into them local materials and climates as well as a community's identity. To build in these standardized ways not only took advantage of this long experience but also reflected a pride in community, a willingness to build in ways that their forebears had used, rather than to express their separation from the community by building something unusual. Yet even so, there is a great deal of diversity within this established framework; compare the French village with a modern subdivision!

Vernacular architecture is increasingly being studied, most notably by Bernard Rudofsky and Christopher Alexander. Rudofsky has written books with titles such as *Architecture Without Architects* and *Streets for People*, and Alexander has intimately described how houses were designed and built in two books, *The Timeless Way of Building* and *A Pattern Language*. He speaks of builders and owners laying out a house right on the ground, marking out the walls where they will stand and modifying construction as the building proceeds in response to the wishes of the owner or to take advantage of a particularly nice glimpse toward the garden. More than any other books, Alexander's give a feeling for how traditional craftsmen were able to make small houses comfortable and efficient, as well as attractive and emotionally satisfying.

The materials most often used in traditional houses were of mineral origin rather than wood. Permanence was all important in societies with a strong sense of family and continuity. Fireproof materials were also important when houses were clustered close together. Stone was preferred, but without stone a stout frame of well-seasoned wood could be erected—a "half-timbered" house—and filled with a number of different materials: rubble, sticks and mud, or brick, which in the past could not be fired at high enough temperatures to stand by itself. In many parts of the world, earth alone was used in different forms, often quite satisfactorily except where earthquakes occurred. Earthen walls were always built with great thickness, which gave them structural stability and acted as a buffer against temperature changes outside, leaving the inside temperatures more uniform. (Glass and insulation would greatly improve the ability to regulate these temperatures, gaining more inside heat in winter and, in the summer storing more of the coolness of the night in the walls.)

Slate was the preferred material for roofs, as in the village on the Loire. Because slate had to be brought from distant mines, it was costly for people who did not benefit from waterborne transportation, such as on the Loire. Tiles also were fired for a permanent roof, but where these materials were not available, thatch was widely used. A thatched roof was not permanent or fireproof, but it was made from an abundant local material and provided insulation. Architects speak of it as the perfect roof from a design perspective, wrapping the house in a warm, thick blanket—just what a roof is supposed to do.

Windows were small in old houses because of the high cost of glass. They were placed carefully so that someone could enjoy the morning sunlight streaming through the window on a winter's day or could visit with passers-by on the street. Since houses often doubled as workplaces, windows were placed so as to light the work. One of the requirements established by guilds was that craftsmen had to do their work in front of a window facing the sidewalk to ensure that proper materials and workmanship were used. Not only was this a pleasant place for the craftsman to work, watching the life on the street outside, but it was interesting for people passing by to see the work being done.

In old towns and cities the houses and shops are almost universally all "crowded together." Generally we do not like squeezing so many people into a small space, and prefer more grass and trees. But high density has many significant advantages. First, it means the economic use of resources: less land is used, common walls insulate the sides of houses and reduce heating needs, and the absence of front yards and spaces at the sides of houses means there is less watering and gardening to do (yet the world of nature is still closer than in sprawling suburban areas). Second, high density means that transportation can be largely on foot, not only eliminating the need for costly alternative modes of transportation but sustaining small shops and making the streets safe places for children to play, quiet and free from fumes. And third, social life is much richer under the conditions high densities create:

there are people on the streets to talk to, shopkeepers to chat with, neighbors sitting in their doorways to greet, and it is never far to meeting places or the town square, the center of social life.

There are also a number of advantages in having social life in public places rather than in the home. It is easy to simply walk out into the social world of a town or a village whenever desired, whether for fifteen minutes or a whole afternoon or evening. It is pleasurable to wander over to the square, sit down with friends over a beer or cup of coffee, join a group playing a game, listen to a dispute, poke around a public market, perhaps buy something for the evening's meal, or just sit and watch the world go by. There is very little opportunity to do this in our society, where social life is concentrated in the home or in private activities. To entertain in the home requires formal arrangements, since just dropping in on people is no longer as acceptable as it once was. Having friends over means calling beforehand to invite them, cleaning the house, and making preparations to have food and drink on hand. And then there is also the concern that perhaps the invited guests would have prefered a quiet evening at home, but did not feel they could decline gracefully. An overloaded social calendar is not possible with social life occurring in public places since the only reason people go there is if they are in the mood to see other people, and there is no need to clean the house or make other preparations. This gives social life a spontaneity and an easy naturalness. What it does not provide is exclusivity; everyone in the community can join if they wish.

The pollsters report that a good many Americans yearn to live in a small town, but our small towns have very few of the attributes of the French village. The attractions of a small town for us are often that they allow us to have more space and to live further away from our neighbors. Near cities, they are often exclusive places for successful people, the ones who have the least need for community. Since we have always had plenty of land, there has been no need to cluster, and we had little interest in it anyway. Our homes are meant to reflect our individuality and our achievements rather than our membership in a community. Abandoned this way, communities have deteriorated to the point where they are seen as a hostile element, as something that can only interfere with our private interests rather than something that adds to our lives. As long as we hold to these values, we will not be able to enjoy the pleasures, the convenience, the efficiencies, and the closeness—to people as well as to the countryside—that characterizes traditional settlement patterns.

A Valley

A gentle valley, such as the one in England shown in the photograph on page 170 is a desirable place for human habitation because of the wide array of useful things such a diverse landscape provides. The stream that flows through the valley, even a small one, can be used for transportation, to power a mill, and for fishing by building small dams and locks. The well-watered meadows close to the stream are considered the best for pasture and haymaking, and the thick roots of the grass protect the soil and stream banks from erosion. The roots also catch the nutrients that may have escaped the best efforts of the farmers to keep them on their fields. (One definition of pollution is a resource out of place; a polluted stream means less fertile soil.) Away from the stream, the drier bottomlands are usually well suited for the cultivation of grains, called the staff of life because they are so nutritious and can be used in so many ways, from bread to

A gentle valley in England. (*Photo credit: The British Tourist Authority.*)

beer. As the land begins to rise above the bottomlands, there will be less danger from late spring frosts, so orchards and vineyards can be safely planted. The well-drained slopes are also where towns and villages are most apt to be built, not only to leave the best lands for crops but to leave the roads drier during the winter, perhaps also to take advantage of a southern exposure for winter sunlight. Manures from the barns go into the kitchen gardens that surround the town, and any nutrients leached away by the rains drain toward the bottomlands, where they are most likely to be caught. Higher up the hillsides are woods for timber and firewood, springs or small streams for gravity-fed water supplies, and rough pastures for animals.

Every piece of land is used, and to its best potential; in this respect, the valley is a utilitarian landscape. But it is also an attractive landscape, the kind of place tourists visit. With its diversity, it provides many different niches for wild flowers, birds, and animals. And with proper care, it can remain productive indefinitely. In many cases, the productivity of such landscapes has actually been improved by human activity, by the draining of wet soils, the removal of tangled vegetation, the planting of grasses and legumes that improved the soil, and the construction of terraces to protect hillside soils and make them more useful. This is man in harmony with nature, working with it, rather than against it.

Other landscapes, of course, have been damaged by improper use; the record is by no means perfect. The hills of the Mediterranean region, denuded of trees and overgrazed, are frequently mentioned. But for the most part, even the Mediterranean region, with all the difficulties this landscape presents, has been made productive. This is no small achievement given the fact that there is virtually no rain during the summer growing season, and there are many hills but few good level soils. To use this landscape a great deal of human labor was needed, especially to build terraces and provide water, and the number of crops that could be grown was limited. Even so, after thousands of years of use, the Mediterranean landscape is still productive, and still attracts painters, something few modern landscapes do.

Even in overpopulated countries, such as China and Japan, traditional man/land systems could still produce beautiful and productive landscapes. The higher population densities, however, required far larger inputs of human labor to maintain them. There was rarely enough feed for draft animals, so more human labor had to be used. Wood was scarce, so materials such as rice straw had to be used for cooking. Two crops had to be squeezed from the land, requiring more intensive effort and a greater risk that one crop might fail. And the heaviest task of all was maintaining the fertility of the soil under such intensive cultivation. All wastes had to be assiduously collected and quickly composted to be used again, rather than being collected in barns to be fed to animals as needed. The fact that high populations could be supported is in itself an achievement, but the labor requirements grew onerous, and the ecological risks increased also, especially today as machines and industrial technology, which are not as gentle with the land as human hands, are increasingly used.

The collection and reuse of wastes is at the core of traditional agricultural systems. Nutrients, once lost, could not be replaced easily without the chemical fertilizers we have today. This caused the countryside to be clean, since everything was put back into the land, but it also caused problems, especially when populations were high; the mountains of China were denuded as farmers turned trees and shrubs into green manure to add nutrients to their soil.

The ideal way to recycle vegetable wastes, such as straw, the inedible parts of vegetables, weeds, leaves, and winter cover crops, is through animals. Cows, pigs, sheep, goats, and poultry will not only process these materials into manure, but in so doing will divert some of the nutrients and energy into foods, for example, meat, dairy products, and eggs; into useful materials such as cloth and leather; and into services —pulling plows and wagons. The alternatives, of composting or mulching, require that the farmer does the work, rather than the animals, and he does not receive the products and the services of the animals. The only reason for doing it this way is if there is not enough food to support animals all year long. Animals are also able to graze hills that are too steep or lands that are too rocky or dry to cultivate and would otherwise be of little use. In India, the sacred cows provide a number of important services—labor for plowing and transport, animal protein in the form of milk, dung for cooking and fertilizer, and scavenging—even though the animals are not killed and eaten, as Westerners regularly recommend (forgetting the central position of nonviolence in Hindu beliefs).

Trees also have an important role that goes well beyond the provision of fuel and building materials. Trees are a source of fertility, since their roots penetrate into the ground to bring up nutrients. Tree roots give off materials that, in a complex process with various fungi, actually take minerals out of rock to support their growth; in this sense, trees make their own fertilizer, bringing it to the surface where it is available to us. Ash from fires and leaf litter becomes an important soil supplement. When populations grow too large, however, trees, like animals, often are squeezed out.

The population of preindustrial Europe was low enough that land could be devoted to woods, but still, its population was high enough to make management necessary. The most intensive form of management was known as *coppice and standard.* Some trees were allowed to grow large for use as building timbers—the standards—while below them the smaller trees—the coppice—were cut regularly for firewood at the ground. The coppice trees were selected for their ability to sprout vigorously from the stump after being cut. The branches grew back rapidly because the tree roots did not have to be regenerated each time; all growth went into the branches. Coppice and standard woods were efficient also because the several layers of branches—from high in the air to close to the ground—intercepted a very substantial part of the sunlight available.

A similar technique was used in trees planted along roads, except there the firewood was harvested some eight to ten feet above the ground so as not to obstruct passage along the road. Known as *pollarding,* this left attractive rows of trees along country roads with large knots out of which the branches grew. It was efficient because it collected the sunlight that would otherwise have been wasted on the road and provided summer shade for travelers as well. It was functional, both ecologically and economically, and attractive as well.

The use of land was also integrated with the spiritual life of the people, investing the lives of people with beauty and significance. The great festivals marked the passage of the year: Christmas on the darkest day of the year, reflecting the hope of new life; Easter, the joyous festival of spring and the renewal of life; Rogantide, when the fields were blessed by the priest; and Lammas, when the first loaf of bread from the harvest was placed on the altar. The land that nourished the physical life also nourished the spiritual life.

Traditional peoples did not understand the workings of nature in a scientific sense. It was only through long experience, and undoubtedly many errors and mistakes, that they learned how to fit their lives into the ways of nature, and to do so in aesthetically and spiritually satisfying ways. These remarkable achievements are usually ignored by conservationists, who are more concerned with natural environments, and by scientists, who consider them primitive. But they are ways that have stood the test of time, and they will be increasingly valued as careful husbandry of land becomes more important to us.

A City

We will have fossil fuels for a long time to come, but even in the dim and distant future when the last of the coal is gone, we will still have many technological advantages over peoples in the past. A horse-drawn mower can do the work of many scythe-wielding harvesters, and a wood-fired threshing machine could thresh an entire village's grain in a day or two rather than beating it with flails for weeks. Because of this, cities will undoubtedly be more a part of our lives in the future than in the past, even with the worst of all resource scenarios. And here again, the past provides us with valuable lessons—how to make them efficient in the material sense, satisfying socially, and attractive as well. The stream of gifts continues.

Venice is not an ordinary city by any stretch of the imagination, but it is particularly useful for our purposes here because it is so well preserved and is such a good place to experience what cities were like before they had to make room for cars. And it is a magical city too, one that is on almost everyone's list of favorite places. Yet there is hardly a touch of green anywhere, except in the flowerpots on the windowsills; it is wall-to-wall stone and people. Venice forces us to think more carefully of just what it is that causes people to love a city, to be loyal to it, to protect it and defend it from change.

Venice was the largest city of Europe during the medieval era because it was the main trading center for goods coming to Europe from the east; the waters of the Adriatic Sea offered protection from the Moslems who controlled the rest of the Mediterranean. The low-lying islands at the head of the Sea were not well suited for a city and required large amounts of stone for foundations and for building up the banks of the waterways that laced the islands (and which became the canals of today). But Venice was wealthy because of its strategic location, and trading centers are always cosmopolitan because of the foreign ideas that come in with foreign goods. The fortunes of Venice waxed and waned, but the stones remain, and they still support a rich panoply of life.

At the top of the photograph of Venice on page 177 is the Piazza San Marco, one of the finest public spaces in the world. But the rest of the city is actually more pertinent to our interests here because its qualities are more common in older European cities.

The main part of Venice is only one mile across, which means that to walk across the entire city takes only half an hour or so. To walk into the center of the city from the periphery takes only fifteen minutes. The permanent population of Venice has been dropping for years as apartments have been converted into tourist facilities, so it is rather arbitrary to give a specific population figure. But in 1950, just before the biggest tourist boom began, it was 191,000. An American city of the same population would cover some *forty times* as much area, assuming a typical population density of 5,000 persons per square mile, and a car would be necessary to travel between points that in Venice can be reached quickly

Venice. Piazza San Marco is at the top of the photograph. (*Photo credit: Charles E. Rotkin, Photography for Industry.*)

and easily on foot. High density makes it possible to avoid the traffic, the jangled nerves, the accidents, the noise, the air pollution, and the cost, both to the traveler and to the government, of cars. In its place are pleasurable walks past shops amid the sounds of people's voices rather than of traffic. When Thoreau wrote "The swiftest traveler is he that goes afoot," he was saying that it takes more time to earn the money for a train ticket than it does to walk the trip. But in Venice, movement is quick even without a ticket! It is a spectacular illustration of the advantages of high density.

Venice has many small squares. They are common in most older cities of Europe, but particularly so in Italy. In Venice, they were the centers of once separate villages that are now different neighborhoods. The narrow streets of the city open out onto these bright, sunlit spaces. In the winter, life congregates on the sunny side; in summer, on the shady sides and the streets. The square is the place where mothers can come with their children, working people can eat their lunch, old people can sit and reminisce, youngsters can play ball, young people can observe the opposite sex, and lovers can meet. The wealthiest people are the ones who can afford to live in the center of all this life, and the poorer people must be satisfied with the periphery.

On certain days of the week, the squares come alive with market stalls full of fresh produce and many other goods under gaily covered canvas. It is a job to move these in, set them up, and remove them at the end of each market day, but in this way small merchants are able to compete with those who can afford to rent the expensive shop space on the square, and the low costs of stalls means that products can be sold at cheaper prices. A flat, stone surface becomes a place of virtually unlimited uses.

The streets that wander through Venice are narrow, but

this is not unusual. The pattern of use varies all day—deliveries in the morning, shoppers and people at work in the daytime, people out for a stroll in the evening, talking with friends, window-shopping, or stopping for a cup of coffee. This is multiple use at its best—commerce, social life, transportation, recreation; in the past, it included production and political activity. Yet the streets are remarkably quiet and pleasant, without the roar of cars that dominates the sounds of our cities or the fumes.

Americans tend to be repelled by the thought of such high densities and an environment devoid of anything green and living. But high density means not only that less land falls under the bulldozer but also that the countryside remains much closer than in a city with low density. Foregoing green spaces in the city—green spaces that are contrived at best—keeps the city from spilling out and obliterating the more authentic green spaces around the city. Our urge to have nature close to us has inadvertently led to the destruction of nature. Italian cities tell us that a city should be a city and the country should be the country, and to try to have the best of both in a city debases both, making cities neither urban nor rural.

Man and Nature in the Industrial Era

One of the saddest legacies of the industrial revolution in England is that cities became symbols of ugliness and economic oppression—of powerful interests that drove people from farms and villages into damp and cramped quarters in sooty cities and into long hours of factory work at poor wages. The result was, inevitably, a hostility toward cities, a hostility that was brought to this country by the early English immigrants who shaped our culture so heavily. It infused

Americans with a yearning for a world dominated by benign nature rather than predatory man, of yeoman farmers and town meetings rather than factory owners and tenements. Thomas Jefferson's agrarian ideal reflected American yearnings, but it did not have the power to stop industrialization; all it did was to cause us to try to make our homes rural enclaves in the city, something that has become increasingly unsuccessful as the urban age evolved.

Now we are dependent on cars for almost everything, including to get away from cities and into contact with nature. But it is necessary to drive long distances to do this, and even when the most carefully preserved areas are reached—the state and national parks, for example—there are large numbers of other people wishing to visit them too, and the campgrounds are crowded, often like small cities themselves. And nature, rather than being comforting to us, can be disturbing. As isolated as we now are from nature, we do not know how to respond to it. We have heard about the intense spiritual experiences others have had in nature, but most visitors to national parks are unsure what to do after seeing the main sights—the highest waterfall, the biggest trees, or the magnificent views. The curio shops seem more comfortable, as do the campgrounds, where we can set up elaborate equipment and try to relax from our hectic lives. But few Americans have the capacity to look deeply into nature and draw satisfactions out of it, in the way we can draw from science, business, sports, or politics, things that are more characteristic of our activist society.

One response is to push further into untrammeled nature, into the wilderness, to try to get completely away from the works of man. But still there is the problem of overuse. Reservations must often be made beforehand, the cutting of firewood for campfires is increasingly prohibited, camping is restricted to established sites, and pit toilets must be installed near popular lakes to make sure the water in the lake is safe.

The number of visitors to parks and wilderness areas is, at best, only a fraction of the total population, and a visit is of necessity a brief escape from a world we have built ourselves but do not feel comfortable in. It is a world that is increasingly dominated by the works of man, almost in mockery of our efforts to do just the opposite—to maintain some ties with nature.

On a theoretical basis it seems that it should be possible to strike a balance between industrial society and nature, but this balance has been very hard to find, not only in this country but anywhere in the world. Even in Japan, where the appreciation of nature and the aesthetic sense are both highly developed, industrialism looks much the same, even worse in some respects. Is it possible that only in traditional societies can such a balance be obtained, with towns and villages surrounded by well-tended fields, pastures, and woods, with only a few larger cities? Such a broad generalization hardly seems justifiable, but industrial civilization has little to offer to counter it. Even the finest private environments are sustained, in a very real sense, by dammed rivers, strip mines, and logged-over lands somewhere else.

It is offensive to turn virgin redwood forests into backyard fences and to drown canyons of red Navajo sandstone to generate electricity for air conditioners. But even though there may be alternatives to some of these uses, the war against nature will continue and even escalate as long as the industrial economy remains so dependent on raw materials to keep people employed, businesses prosperous, and tax revenues coming in. Our economy is based on the heavy-handed use of nature, and even though nature has magnificent recuperative powers, the recovery (however and whenever it may occur) is unlikely to match the beauty and the wholeness of the original environment. In the meantime, the natural environments that have been destroyed to build what is so often ugly has led to a form of self-hatred—or seeing humankind as a cancerous growth on a once beautiful planet. In the process, we have gone from seeing nature as wild and dangerous to seeing it as a refuge from an oppressive modern society.

The reasonable position between these two extremes is there for us to see: It is the human landscape that is our surest gift from the past. It is available to us to emulate, with a population at once decentralized but clustered, creating not only a rural renaissance, but an urban renaissance as well. Even with simple material standards, individuals would be able to choose from a wide range of places to work and live, from isolated woods to small towns to bustling cities. This is all possible, and it would take less work to build than it would take to sustain industrial civilization, a task that will, in time, become impossible. But this involves change, and change is usually resisted, at least until all efforts to sustain a known way of life have failed.

There is one exception, however, one way in which fundamental change can come quickly. Religious conversion has the power to radically reorder the way people see the world. This will seem alien to many readers, but it is already occurring as people grow disillusioned with the kind of society that has grown out of a rational, scientific view of reality.

10

Religion, the Hardest Step

A world view shaped by religious belief is the main alternative to a world view shaped by reason and science, the dominant form of understanding today. For centuries now, there have been many who argue that we do not need religion at all, while others, such as Jung, claim that human beings need both, and that when we empty ourselves of religious belief, "the vacuum gets filled with absurd political and social ideas, which one and all are distinguished by their spiritual bleakness." The emotional richness of the age of faith—the medieval era—contributed to its being the longest period of peace and stability in Western history. And just as medieval villages and market towns are parts of our heritage, so too are the religious experiences that helped shape them. The question we must now take on is: Can this religious heritage be useful to us again in the future?

Traditional societies did not reject reason in favor of religious explanations for all of life; reason was essential within a very large frame of reference. But there was a level of understanding that reason could not reach, an area of higher truths that people were brought to by the world's great religious teachers, and from these truths flowed ethical systems that shaped the world people lived in, that gave it form, texture, and color. Religion, in this sense, can be seen as adding to what science can provide. The goal of science is to *describe* reality; religion attempts to give it *meaning*, and to order life around this meaning. *And while it is difficult for many people in this day and age to find religious faith, it is still possible to accept the ethical systems that religions developed in order to halt the tragedy of the commons that is spreading through our society.* Imagine, for example, that there were communities organized on the principles of the world's great faiths. How many people would choose one of them compared to the world we live in? Not an insignificant number, I would expect, but such alternatives are not available (although a number are being worked on). As time passes, however, and the aridity of modern society is joined by economic distress, the ancient organizing force of religion will increasingly be relevant to our hopes and aspirations for the future. This is occurring already.

The interest in religion today is not in returning to the religious unity of the Middle Ages; that is neither possible nor desirable. *The goal is much more prosaic: It is simply a way to help us get by, a way to resist the spreading meaninglessness of modern society. Religion can help people overcome their self-centeredness and to become part of a larger, more complete whole than is possible in today's fragmented, individualistic society.* Rather than being an issue of reason versus faith, the question is how to use *both* to create the good life. It is not an easy question; religion is indeed the hardest step.

But reason has been hard on us too.

The Folly of Playing God

Beginning with the Renaissance, Western civilization was able to take the rational process ahead so spectacularly that, not surprisingly, we came to feel that we did not need the truths that religion had to offer. Further, because religious beliefs could not be proven scientifically, and in some instances contradicted scientific understanding, they were widely judged to be contrary to scientific reality and therefore untrue, at best the result of inadequate knowledge, at worst of superstition and fear. Religion was seen as a crutch that modern man no longer needed. And indeed, science and technology have shaped our society to the point where the size and complexity of industrial society virtually *demands* an objective understanding of material reality, and this is true whether a country is capitalist or communist, Christian or atheist.

But a good part of American society has an active antipathy to religion that runs much deeper than the fact that it is simply inadequate to the needs of technological society, and this antipathy is based on very real and very bitter historical experiences. To many people today, religion means centuries of wars in which Christians killed Christians and non-Christians with equal fervor; of intolerance, guilt, and fear; of hypocrisy, fraud, and humbug. The constitutional separation of church and state has wide public support; by default, reason has become the "established orthodoxy" of our society. But the constitutional protection of religious freedom also gives communities organized on a religious basis much greater flexibility than secular communities, a not insignificant advantage.

The historical experience of Christianity is a major obstacle to many people today, but history has treated the humanists no better. The hopes of a world of peace and brotherhood have been disappointed. Rather than mutual understanding and respect between peoples and between nations, we have instead a world bristling with guns and hostilities, our nation being no exception. In retrospect, it must be deemed wishful thinking to have expected that reason and science would only be used for the betterment of mankind and not by the greedy and the ambitious as well, not by Hitler to build buzz bombs and gas chambers, not by nations to develop nuclear bombs and chemical and biological weapons, not by corporations to profit from the sale of shoddy goods or by sophisticated white-collar criminals trying to get their hands on such profits. What basis is there for individuals, groups, or nations to restrain themselves from using science and reason for their own purposes? Reason, in fact, is what pushes them to do these things which are in their immediate interests. *It is this quality of calculated self-interest that has come to characterize the age of reason, rather than peace and brotherhood.* It has produced a world in which there is little that can be counted on and few who can be trusted. The important point, however, is that *this all makes sense from the point of view of the rational, scientific way of seeing the world,* a way of seeing in which nothing is sacred. It cannot be blamed on a breakdown in our political processes, educational system, or the family.

There were premonitions of this oncoming barrenness of modern life even among those who were its precursors. In *The Brothers Karamazov,* Dostoevsky wrote that if the belief in immortality were destroyed "nothing then would be immoral, everything would be permissible," and "every living force maintaining the life of the world would dry up." Nietzsche predicted the advent of nihilism as an "inevitable result of rationalism and calculation," which would destroy "unreflective spontaneity." In Nietzsche's view, Socrates began the process, that "despotic logician" whose "great Cyclops eye" of rational consciousness never "glowed with the artist's divine frenzy," whose "voice always spoke to dissuade." Nietzsche pities "all, who like myself, suffer from the great loathing, for whom the old God died and no new God yet lieth in cradles and napkins." Even Marx spoke of it in *The Communist Manifesto:* "The Bourgeoisie, wherever it has got the upper hand, has put an end to all feudal, idyllic relations. It has left remaining no other nexus between man and man than naked self-interest, than callous 'cash payment.' It has drowned the most heavenly ecstasies of religious fervor, of chivalrous enthusiasm, of philistine sentimentalism, in the icy waters of egotistical calculation."

There is still the feeling, however, that if we just made some changes in the way we did things, we could capitalize on the great advances we have made through reason and science and build a society that matches our technological achievements and reflects a truly modern consciousness. But so many good ideas have only led to disappointment. A recurring theme is socialism; it has been expressed in many ways, often with truly inspired literature—of people working together to enjoy the benefits of technology rather than being run over by it in a no-holds-barred struggle to get rich. It sounded so good, good enough to attract many of the best minds of the nineteenth century, but who would have expected that it would instead lead to societies where the competition simply shifted from the marketplace to the bureaucracies that characterize them? Similarly, the human potential movement made such good sense when it was first introduced, but ended up simply as a new form of self-indulgence in a society with an excess of it. All the positivistic solutions that are characteristic of the scientific approach have, if not failed, served to reduce people, even as it was claimed that man was the measure of all things. With the transcendental truths gone, the existential void opened up that has been so debilitating to serious writers and has caused so much of modern art to be cold and empty or to foretell the senseless violence that has plagued this age.

Yet we don't like to admit that we are out of new ideas, and indeed there are all sorts of promoters around filling the demand for new breakthroughs. Their ideas, however, if not rehashes of old ones, are new ones that reflect more our cultural diseases than anything else, the science-fiction hope that space travel will provide the openings our ambitions desperately need, or the popular psychology movement, which offers all sorts of shortcuts to the personal power and self-knowledge people are looking for so desperately. For most people, however, there is only a spreading disillusionment with the emptiness of secular society, and it is this disillusionment that has generated a renewed interest in religion.

The role of religion in traditional society, however, whether in our own past or other societies today, is more demanding than we tend to expect.

Integration—The Cultural Function of Religion

The evolution of the human brain left homo sapiens—man the thinker—incomplete. No longer were instincts an adequate guide to behavior, as they are for animals. Our brains demanded answers to many questions, but the most insistent question was—and still is—What is the meaning of life?

Meaninglessness is difficult to live with, and the world's great religions are the ones that, over the centuries, have provided the most profound and enduring answers to this question, answers that give a purpose to life. *But the genius of these religious explanations is that they also served to mold conflicting individuals into a harmonious group*, into a band or tribe initially, then into a body of believers, and later into a trans-national force that strove to make brothers of all men.

The integration provided by religion thus has two elements, a *vertical* element, which strives to answer the age-old questions of the meaning of life, and a *horizontal* element, which shapes an often defiant and unruly human nature into a moral community.

Vertical Integration. The scientific advances of the modern era have, in a sense, made the questions of the meaning of life more oppressive, for we now have excellent evidence of our insignificance. Each of us is indeed very small compared to the immensity of the earth, let alone the infinitude of space. As a single individual, we are lost among the billions of people on the earth. Our alloted life span is short and only an instant in geologic time. Is life what Shakespeare suggests through Macbeth?

> *. . . a poor player*
> *That struts and frets his hour upon the stage,*
> *And then is heard no more; it is a tale*
> *Told by an idiot, full of sound and fury,*
> *Signifying nothing.*

Is there no larger purpose to life than immediate gratification, or the pursuit of wealth and power?

But while science has made the answers harder, in another

sense it has made them more profound. Each scientific advance seems to generate ever larger questions than those answered, whether in the nature of the universe, the human body, or the atom, to create ever greater mysteries and to make nature even more awe inspiring. Darwin's theory of evolution was a great advance in understanding how the biological world came to exist in its present form, but it is still a rough, mechanistic explanation that falls far short of explaining the incredible beauty of nature. Indeed, it does not even try to explain, for example, why a seagull should be so graceful for its base function of scavenging, or why the coloring of flowers and birds should be so ordered and harmonious. The survival of the fittest obviously has truth to it, but it is a small, smug truth compared to the wholeness of life. It says nothing about the joy of seeing a smile on a loved one's face or the exhilaration of a summer thunderstorm. The miracle of life in all its incredible diversity is more than great enough to make the heart sing, and human life is very much a part of that miracle. These are the transcendental matters that science has no tools to deal with.

The whole thrust of scientific understanding has been toward the easier questions of "how" things work, rather than the "why," which are the more insistent ones as well as the ones that science has no special means of handling. But even the understanding of how things work is beyond our capacities. We do not understand the workings of photosynthesis—the process by which plants fix the life-giving sunlight on which all life depends. Scientists can describe what seems to be going on and can influence it with chemicals and knives, but even with the sophisticated knives of the gene splicers, fundamental understanding evades us. The claims that scientists are close to understanding the origins of life are in fact arrogant speculations. The achievements of science should not be denigrated; they are magnificent. But if we cannot fully understand natural processes that are going on around us today, how is it possible to explain the origins of life billions of years ago?

Traditional people have fewer dreams of omniscience, of being able to understand and control everything. The world is amazing enough for them—the seasons following each other, seeds pushing their way up through the soil each spring, and the beauty of the flowers and birds. Human beings are a part of this world, a world that is given a luminous quality by faith. The world is ordered, given a sense of justice, and endowed with hope, even in death. To the degree the answers are good ones, life is infused with meaning and significance. The individual is integrated into the oneness of life. These too are magnificent achievements.

Horizontal Integration. But vertical integration is only half the task, for little would be gained if there was a great gulf between these transcendental truths and an everyday world full of torment and ugliness. Religion, to be effective, had to get down to the nitty-gritty, down to the age-old struggles and conflicts of people living and working together. It had to make life on earth a verification of religious beliefs, rather than a contradiction of them.

The only practical assumption about human nature is that people have tendencies toward good as well as bad. Religion's role is to encourage what it deems to be the good and discourage the bad. Every religion establishes a set of rules, justifies them on religious grounds, and asks for obedience. "Thou shalt not" murder, steal, cheat, lie, or commit adultery are almost universal prohibitions, ones that long experience has shown to be necessary to permit the smooth progression of human life. Moreover, they must be backed up by sanctions.

The threat of supernatural punishment is not attractive to us in this liberated era, but such sanctions are part of what gives religious systems their power to organize society, and it is striking how effective the threat of punishment in the afterlife has been through the ages in the absence of any proven ability to carry out such threats. The Latin root of the word *religion* is *religare*, which means to bind, and now that we are free of the binding force of a deity who can see into our hearts we are doing things that we would not have done before. As the self-control that stemmed from the fear of divine retribution has ceased to be effective, we have had to increase the external controls—laws, regulations, and police—but these can be avoided so much more easily than an all-seeing deity.

The main thrusts of most faiths, however, the ones that give them their distinguishing character, are the positive admonitions of love, charity, service, hope, forgiveness, and humility. Every religion has its counterparts to the golden rule and the cardinal virtues of Christianity. To the degree they are followed with good heart, the individual becomes a part of a community and enjoys its respect. To the degree economics, politics, and other institutions are made to reflect religious ideals, they too are sanctified and made a part of the moral community, and not alien to it. The result is horizontal integration.

The question to ask, then, is *What could be more important to the good life than to live in a community where such vertical and horizontal integration existed?* It would have to be both comforting and ennobling for individuals as well as providing a sound basis for community. Such integration is something that we are certainly very far from in our society. For the most part, each of us is left to achieve our own vertical integration, something we are finding difficult to do. The family, bolstered by its biological role and the instincts that go with it, provides a valuable element of centeredness, but society calls insistently in other directions. We are presented with a secular challenge, one that is in broad conflict with our Judeo-Christian heritage. It is a difficult time to follow the words of the Sermon on the Mount, the core of Christ's teachings of love and selflessness.

This is nothing new, however. The history of Western civilization can be seen as a struggle between a youthful, active, creative, but often violent Western mind and a Christianity that periodically falls into the same trap. It has been a difficult history but one that is important because of the insights it provides about our situation today, particularly about why religion has become so problematic.

Christianity and Western Civilization

Will Durant suggested that cultures can be known by the individuals they honor. In China, the sage, the man of quiet wisdom, is honored. In India, it is the saint, with Gandhi the modern example. In the West, it is the man of action. Alexander the Great, the warrior king whose main achievement was to spread Greek civilization as far as India, provides a good example. But he did it by the sword, spreading death and destruction all along the way, and dying at age thirty-seven. The ancient civilizations of the West were modern in many respects—intellectually active, youthful in energy, and highly creative. But many of their achievements were based on military power, slavery, and exploitation. And because this is an unstable basis for a civilization, they were usually brief; Periclean Greece lasted only a few decades before the city-states that Athens had subjugated rose up in revolt.

The Roman Empire lasted longer because it backed up its

military achievements with strong administration. But internal decay eventually led to the Dark Ages, which gave Christianity a chance to try its hand in organizing Western society. The church, like Western civilization in general, survived by the skin of its teeth during this period, and then it took many centuries for the missionaries to overcome the anarchy of the Dark Ages by converting the barbarians to Christianity, turning them into good Europeans—Franks, Lombards, Goths, Saxons, and Norsemen. With conversion, the authority of the Roman Catholic church was established. The Dark Ages slowly gave way to the medieval era.

The medieval era is a unique period in Western civilization, not only because it is the only time when religion was the organizing force, but also because of its long period of relative peace and stability. The proud, restless nature of Western man was held down—although never completely—by the church, as well as by the catastrophe of the Dark Ages. The church established a community, a united Christendom, to which all could gain admittance. Feudal ties were approved by the church in return for the submission of the feudal lords to the church's authority; even kings had to submit. The guilds were sanctioned in return for controls on their activities. Usury was banned, as the Bible required, and commerce was suspect; anything that produced a profit on someone else's labor was deemed wrong. Labor was honored, but the appetite for wealth was curbed; both avarice and sloth were included in the list of the seven deadly sins. Everywhere, economic interests were subordinated to the real business of life, of salvation. The central role of faith in medieval society is best illustrated by the gothic cathedrals pointing heavenward, daring architectural and engineering achievements with their soaring naves and flying buttresses, dwarfing the houses and shops that clustered around them. In the eleventh and twelfth centuries, nobles joined peasants in carrying stones from the quarries to help build them. This was the age of faith.

But as the centuries passed, the successes of the Middle Ages slowly led to difficulties. The Crusades not only provided an outlet for a long suppressed spirit of adventure and conquest, but they opened much of the Mediterranean to trade, and this led to the reemergence of commerce with the East and contact with new ideas. Bankers in Italian city-states grew wealthy and patronized the arts generously. The Western mind grew more confident, stimulated by the translation of Greek and Roman texts, and it began to shake off the medieval restraints. The church itself was inevitably drawn into the heady experience of the Italian Renaissance; it too became worldy and wealthy. The election of the pope became enmeshed in politics that were to inspire Machiavelli. Faith began to give way to the humanism of the Renaissance.

In the rest of Europe to the north, however, the age of faith still reigned, especially in the villages and towns where most of the population lived. But trade was spreading to the growing cities of northern Europe too, and the rising commercial classes were threatening farmers and craftsmen alike. And even though most country priests went about their age-old tasks faithfully, others were infected with the spirit of the times and grew ambitious for the powerful posts the church offered, and the funds that could be obtained through selling indulgences and ecclesiastical appointments. Not surprisingly, northern Europe revolted against the unsettling changes spreading from the south, and especially against the authorities in Rome who were supposed to be the shepherds of their flock.

Roman Catholicism was uniquely vulnerable to this kind of breakdown since among the world's major religions it is the only one with the degree of centralization and hierarchical control that came from Rome. This was advantageous in many cases—it is what gave Christendom its unity—but it also meant that Christianity lacked the diversity of Hinduism and Buddhism, for example, where the existence of many different sects meant that if one grew proud and corrupt, the faithful could shift to others, maintaining the continuity and the vitality of the faith. The centralization of Catholicism stemmed from its early history, when the need was to create order out of the anarchy of the Dark Ages. But later, when devout individuals and groups wished to practice their faith in their own ways, the church felt threatened, especially by the mendicant monks, such as Saint Francis, whose poverty and faith were in such contrast to the church's wealth and worldliness. Saint Francis was finally taken into the fold of the church, but many other prophetic groups were harshly suppressed. Even the Eastern church in Constantinople was seen as a threat to Rome's hegemony, and Rome refused to come to its aid when Crusaders sacked it in 1204, a sad conclusion to Constantinople's key role in barring the Moslem tide for centuries. The Roman church had, in effect, become a bureaucracy, concerned more with its own interests than in maintaining the divine order the church had built over the centuries. Bureaucracy, one of the diseases of modern society, was the death of medieval civilization.

The goal of Luther and the other leaders of the Reformation was to purge Christianity of its diseases, but as is so often the case in revolutionary changes, they overreacted. In its zeal, the Reformation rejected much that was at the core of religion—its role of integrating a society through an ethical system. Because of the arrogance of the Roman authorities, Luther made the Bible the only source of authority; no longer would the church act as an intermediary between man and

God, nor could the saints and Mary provide help. Confession was rejected, as well as doing penance to atone for sins; after the Reformation, people would have to live with their sins and the guilt they felt over them. Faith alone became the criterion for salvation, since good works could be contrived for public display. Luther wrote, "As the soul needs the word alone for life and justification, so it is justified by faith alone, and not by any works." The Protestant authorities rejected charity since it had permitted a lack of discipline. They washed their hands of politics in general, leaving the state with greatly expanded power. And although Luther was medieval in his economic thinking, he rejected the church's role in maintaining this economic system, leaving the rising commercial classes with more freedom and, ultimately, with much greater power.

The leaders of the Reformation purified the faith, but they did so with a vengeance. Not only did the Reformation empty the church of much of its social content—its role in horizontal integration—but it isolated individuals in a private relationship with a harsh and severe God, made more difficult because many of the supports of Catholicism were removed—the Mass, the sacred images, the veneration of Mary and the saints, and its music and art—which had given the medieval era its emotional richness. Anything that was considered an unnecessary impediment to a personal relationship with God was rejected; even the bonds of kinship were treated with skepticism, as distracting man from God.

Luther was a religious mystic, with little interest in practical matters of economics and government. Calvin was the revolutionary. He was a member of the prosperous commercial class of Geneva, which had ties with trading centers all over Europe. This class embodied the economic values of thrift, enterprise, and the discipline of low wages to keep the poor from turning into rabble. Calvin integrated the economic values of the middle class into the theology of the Reformation: the main device by which this was accomplished was the concept of predestination—the belief that people were destined for heaven or hell even before they were born.

The Old Testament mentions the term *predestination* briefly, in reference to the much larger matter of God's purpose for humanity, his providence or design. Calvin's use of the term, however, was much more specific; predestination meant that salvation was beyond the ability of an individual to influence; it was foreordained, according to Calvin, that most newborn babies were fated to end up in hell. A more profoundly un-Christian belief is hard to imagine since it denies the Biblical emphasis on individual responsibility as well as the belief that God is merciful and just. Under Calvin, salvation became an exclusive matter for the elect only rather than something to unite the faithful with justice and mercy. What is more extraordinary yet about the doctrine of predestination is that the only way a person could know if they were among the elect was if they were successful economically! The Calvinists who initiated the industrial revolution could put men, women, and children to work for long hours in unhealthy factories, paying them a pittance, and still feel their own prosperity was proof of their salvation, while the miserable existence of the workers only meant that they were destined for hell.

One thing this certainly provided, however, was an overwhelming inducement to work since this was the only way to respond to the anxiety that predestination created of whether one was destined for heaven or hell. And it also led directly to capitalism, since the wealth created in the new factories could not be consumed or used for good works or charity; that is what the Catholics had done. All that could be done with wealth was to reinvest it, and thereby produce more goods in an unending process that ultimately led to today's abundance. This is the definition of capitalism, and even though it has transcended its Calvinist origins, *we are still left with its anxieties and feelings that we are nothing if we are not successful. We still see economic success as salvation, as being among the elect, but on earth now rather than in heaven.*

The Calvinists became the progressive element in Europe and then in North America, keenly proud of the wealth created and the advanced methods by which it was produced. Calvinist discipline soon gave Protestant countries supremacy over the Catholic countries which had initiated the Age of Discovery and had such a head start in accumulating booty from all over the world. But trade and manufacturing were steadier and more secure sources of wealth, and it was trade in slaves and rum that built the prosperity of the attractive seaport towns of New England, activities that were entirely consistent with its Puritan faith. So was the establishment of Harvard College in 1636, just sixteen years after landing at Plymouth Rock, which reflected the intellectual thrust of Puritanism. Calvinism, in effect, provided the religious justification for Protestants to join the worldwide free-for-all for wealth and power. The restless and creative spirit of Western civilization was set free again, but with it came the violence too. We see it as a creative process, but the cultures that were overrun—the slaves taken and the people forced to work in mines and plantations—undoubtedly saw it as brute force of arms.

The transformation from the medieval age of faith and community to the modern age of reason and individualism is the subject of a number of now classic studies. Whether written by historians, such as Tawney's *Religion and the Rise of Cap-*

italism, sociologists, such as Nizbet's *The Quest for Community* and Weber's *Protestantism and the Spirit of Capitalism*, or psychologists, such as Fromm's *Escape from Freedom*, the conclusions are the same; man is left alone and powerless in a cold, uncaring world, and the only way to cope with the anxiety created is through a whirlwind of economic activity. Community is abandoned, the poor are despised, and the providential plan for mankind is revealed only by self-seeking economic activities. Such is the point to which the religion of the Sermon on the Mount has been reduced by Western civilization.

Where Do We Stand Now?

This misalliance between religion and economics, and the degree to which it has been embodied in our cultural life, must be accepted as the central dilemma of our times. We could live with its harshness as long as it was also generating so much wealth and opportunity, but scarcity will leave us with its darker side, its severity, anxiety, and hostility. Economic decline holds real terror for us since there is so little else to fall back on. With community weak and the family under stress, adversity often leaves only the cold bureaucracies to turn to, and even these are being cut back. A society that is organized around "getting and spending" will become a bitter place to live when there is less to get and less to spend.

Because Christianity was so instrumental in the evolution of this system, it is not surprising that the renewed interest in religion has taken many other paths, including a number of new ones. But since religion is something that has occupied people's minds for thousands of years, it is not surprising that the new paths have not gone very far into the complex world of the human spirit. And again, many new religions reflect our sickness more than anything else. Scientology reflects not only the faith in science but Ayn Rand's glorification of selfishness, and the occult reflects the flight from reason.

Not surprisingly, many searchers have gravitated toward the high road of the Eastern faiths. Their greater maturity and sophistication has permitted them to avoid a number of the pitfalls of Christianity, such as the need to explain evil if God is all powerful, the existence of a heaven and hell, and the arrogance of seeing God in the image of man. More importantly, the religions of the East have shown what tolerance is —seeing all religions as different paths to the same end, to be learned from rather than gone to war over. The East has shown that it is possible to conquer with passiveness, and that such conquests are more enduring than conquering with the sword. Contact with the East has inevitably changed our religious perceptions, and Western civilization is unlikely to ever be quite the same.

Yet at the same time, comparisons with the Eastern religions serve to illustrate the unique characteristics of Christianity, primarily its positive admonitions. Selflessness is the great unifying principle of all the world's great religions, but in Christianity it is expressed through love. The core of both Buddhism and Hinduism is the avoidance of suffering by the cessation of desire, while Christ's call to love is direct, even to the point of loving one's enemy. Love is the great commandment, to love God and to love man. John equates love with God, while Paul says "If I have all faith, so as to move mountains, but have not love, I am nothing." Saint Augustine goes so far as to say "Love God, and do as you will." In the Bible, the golden rule is stated positively—"Do unto others as you would have them do unto you"—while in Confucianism, it is phrased negatively—"Do not do unto others what you would not have them do unto you."

But what if the Christian ideal of love is unreachable? Does this give the Eastern faiths greater practical usefulness? It is very difficult to say. Buddhism, for example, has proven itself adaptable in a number of countries in the East where it has been introduced, and this same process could occur in the West. It already has, in a sense, with the growing interest in meditation. Meditation is certainly a useful way to slow people's minds down in this fast-paced society, but as it is used here, the goal of meditation has become the discovery of one's inner self; in the East, the goal is to overcome one's self-centeredness in order to attain oneness with the universal spirit which is the Buddhist concept of divinity. Whether looking into ourselves this way is indeed Buddhism or simply another example of our obsession with ourselves remains to be seen, but the age-old goal of Buddhism—the cessation of desire in order to achieve release from suffering—is alien to the Western mind.

We can certainly learn much from the East, but we must also agree with Jung: "If we try to cover our [spiritual] nakedness with the gorgeous trappings of the East . . . we would be playing our own history false. A man does not sink down to beggary only to pose afterward as an oriental potentate. . . . We are, surely, the rightful heirs of Christian symbolism, but somehow we have squandered our heritage." The goal should be renewal. "Eternal truths need a human language that alters with the spirit of the times."

The question is whether this is possible, given the strong forces that organize our society, forces that are reflected in huge organizations, powerful technology, and rapid mobility, a society that depends on rational self-interest in order to function. There is very little space left in all of this for any ethical system based on religion, regardless of what its character is. There is greatness in all the world's universal faiths, but all of them evolved under conditions that were quite different from those of today; in societies where most work was done by independent farmers and craftsmen, where the size of social organization was small, mobility was low, and technology was simple.

But this is the direction the sustainable economy is heading as economic activity shifts toward renewable resources, simpler technology, population decentralization, and a greater reliance on community. To make all this work, in fact, an ethical system that is appropriate to these emerging conditions will be needed. If the sustainable economy is not to be just the fallout from the industrial economy with the conflict intensified by economic deterioration, then some way must be found to encourage people to accept the obligations necessary to give a community life, and this is the age-old function of religion. Today we think of religion primarily in terms of vertical integration—the answers to the ultimate questions of life—but an *ethic* capable of providing horizontal integration is equally important, perhaps even more so given the immediate need for alternatives to the self-seeking ethic of an overripe industrial system.

Any religion worthy of the name must deal with economics, must somehow infuse this day-to-day activity with its truths. This is especially true in the West because of the dominant role of economics in our society and the perverse role of Christianity in the evolution of capitalism. The Eastern faiths that order large societies, primarily Hinduism and Confucianism, do this in different ways, by reincarnation and caste in the case of Hinduism, and through obligations to ancestors and the emperor in Confucianism. These are unlikely to be very helpful to us. What the Bible says about economics, however, turns out to be surprisingly useful in the context of the emerging sustainable economy. It suggests that, if we can look beyond the historical aberrations of Christianity, there is wisdom to be found in it.

Biblical Economics

Human beings have needs that must be met, and incentives must be provided to meet them. But there must be limits as well, limits on the innate tendency to acquisitiveness if it is not to lead to envy, greed, and exploitation of the weak by the strong. And the equally innate tendency toward helping others and working together must also be encouraged. The ways in which the economics of the Bible reach toward these objectives are interesting. They are also unfamiliar; it is striking how far our actions have diverged from our Judeo-Christian roots.

Wealth. Wealth in the Bible is sometimes a gift of God, a reward for righteousness, but for the most part is is deemed to be a destructive obsession, one that leads to all manner of injustices and to affliction of the poor. In both the Old Testament and the New, there is strong, clear language denouncing the love of wealth for its own sake. "Those who desire to be rich fall into temptation, into a snare, into many senseless and hurtful desires that plunge men into ruin and destruction. For the love of money is the root of all evils." (1 Timothy 6:9–10) The rich who have "grown fat and sleek . . . know no bounds in deeds of wickedness," (Jeremiah 5:27) and because of this they will be punished; "Come now, you rich, weep and howl for the miseries that are coming upon you." (James 5:1) The common admonition is to "Keep your life free from love of money, and be content with what you have." (Hebrews 13:5)

Even when wealth is a gift from God rather than the result

of greed, man should not take pride in it. The wicked man says, "My power and the might of my hand have gotten me this wealth," (Deuteronomy 8:17) rather than giving thanks for it as a gift, as the righteous would do. And for those with wealth, the obligations are clear—*to use this gift for the benefit of all. But there is no call for the general redistribution of wealth; the important things are not material.* "Having food and raiment, let us therewith be content." (1 Timothy 6:8) "Better is a dinner of herbs where love is, than a fatted ox and hatred with it." (Proverbs 15:17) And although Christ expressed deep sympathy with the poor and the needy, and assured them of their blessedness in God's eyes, the ideal was *to have little but to have enough.* The Lord's Prayer asks, "Give us this day our daily bread," and another prayer is ". . . give me neither poverty nor riches; feed me with the food that is needful for me, lest I be full and deny thee, and say, 'Who is the Lord?' or lest I be poor, and steal, and profane the name of my God." (Proverbs 30:8–9)

Work and Charity. Work is a positive value, and there is a direct admonition for everyone to work to provide for their own needs and to help the less fortunate. "Let the thief no longer steal, but rather let him labor, doing honest work with his hands, so that he may be able to give to those in need." (Ephesians 4:28) Paul goes so far as to say "If anyone will not work, let him not eat," (2 Thessalonians 3:10)—*but the poor are to be given the resources necessary to work with*; that is the key difference with the narrow, cold way the Calvinists interpreted Paul's words. And these resources are to be given as a matter of *right*, not as alms to a beggar, which can be withdrawn if the recipient is not properly contrite or humble. Providing people with what they need to work avoids the severe frustration we generate in our society by demanding that everyone work while accepting unemployment in the millions as necessary for the rest of the economy, denying people the chance to be responsible. And then we offer assistance through a welfare system that is demeaning and humiliating. Under the Biblical system, the resources with which to work are to be provided within the context of a community where it can be known who is really in need, something that is not possible to know in a large-scale bureaucratic welfare system.

Not only is there an obligation to help the needy in the Bible, but it is to be done with a good heart. "As the Lord your God has blessed you, you shall give to him" (Deuteronomy 15:14) and "You shall give to him freely, and your heart shall not be grudging when you give to him; because for this the Lord your God will bless you." (Deuteronomy 15:10) In Christ's words, *the Last Judgment is based solely on the help given to those who are hungry, thirsty, naked, sick, and in prison*, for "as you did it to one of these the least of these my brethren, you did it unto me." (Matthew 25:40)

Income Distribution. The requirement that the comfortable help the needy reduces disparities in living standards, but there are other requirements that press this further, especially in the Mosaic code. "When you reap the harvest of your land, you shall not reap your field to its very border, neither shall you gather the gleanings after your harvest. And you shall not strip your vineyard bare, neither shall you gather the fallen grapes of your vineyards; you shall leave them for the poor and for the sojourner." (Leviticus 19:9–10) To borrow money is generally discouraged; "Owe no one anything, except to love one another; for he who loves his neighbor has fulfilled the law." (Romans 13:8) But if adversity strikes, loans are to be provided without interest and without security, and every seventh year, the sabbatical year, all loans are to be forgiven. If a family becomes so poor that it has to sell its land, it cannot be sold in perpetuity, but must be returned in the year of the jubilee, every fiftieth year (after seven sabbaticals, plus a year). When Isaiah charges, "Woe to those who join house to house, who add field to field, until there is no room, and you are made to dwell alone in the midst of the land" (Isaiah 5:8), he is condemning those who own so much land that others cannot support themselves. As the Israelites grew wealthy and powerful, they strayed from the law, and the great reformer was trying to bring them back to it.

Stewardship. Because "the earth is the Lord's and the fullness thereof" (Psalms 24:1), and we are coming to it as strangers and pilgrims, our responsibility is to care for the earth, to replenish it, and to hand this gift on to others in undiminished form. Ownership of the land is thus a concept very different from ours; it is a limited right to use the land for sustenance, but it also carries an obligation to care for the land. Rather than freedom to do anything one wants with land, it was required, for example, that it be rested every seventh year, and that the products of the vines and the pastures were to go to the poor. Yet the right to the land was secure since ownership was considered to be the surest way to encourage good husbandry; it was assumed that the concern for one's children and their children was the strongest basis for preserving the land's productivity. To buy and sell land would abrogate this responsibility. And the family was, of course, the basic economic unit: "Your wife shall be like a fruitful vine within your house; your children shall be like olive shoots around your table." (Psalms 128:3)

Beyond the requirement of stewardship, however, the Bible says little about what we would call conservation, and nature plays little role in the Christian world view, except as a manifestation of God's power and love. For the most part, the ethics of the Bible apply to the relationships between human beings as opposed to the relationships between man and nature. The first chapter of Genesis gives man "dominion over the fish of the sea and over the fowl of the air and over every living thing." (Genesis 1:28) In recent years this has been widely interpreted as leading to the destructive use of nature in the West, a charge for which there is some justification. Nature, in Christianity, does not have a spirit or a soul; it is not a part of all divinity as it is in the Eastern religions, and thus there is less inhibition in taking from nature at will. But at the same time, this argument should not be taken too far. *The one period in Western civilization when Christianity was dominant, the medieval era, was also the time when there was the greatest balance in man's use of the environment.* It was the time when restraints on the accumulation of material things were reinforced by a number of devices designed to provide a sufficiency, but to restrain the excess accumulation that leads to an overexploitation of the environment.

The economic system of the Bible is one that is very difficult to characterize in modern terms; it is neither liberal nor conservative, socialist nor capitalist. It includes private property, but restricts it widely, and goes to great lengths to avoid concentration of wealth. It strives to give individuals and families a measure of economic security by right, and assures everyone a place in the economic life of the community. But most importantly, the economic system of the Bible tells us in this materialistic era that man does not live by bread alone. To have enough is important, but there are other things that are more important to human beings than an unending quest for more.

The Question of Faith

It is regularly asserted that the faith that made such ethical systems work is not possible in this modern age, and that without faith the ethical systems will not work for us. Is faith the barrier that will keep us from being able to use the accumulated wisdom embodied in the world's great religions?

There is little disagreement that faith is difficult for many people today because our way of life has been so dominated by reason and science for generations. But is it not possible that a *rational* decision can be made to use the ethical systems of religion *if it meets people's needs*, if it enables them to work together harmoniously within a community? It would be better, of course, to have the vertical integration that faith provides as well, right from the start. But faith cannot be willed the same way a decision can be taken to adopt an ethical system as a basis for community. Faith is often difficult even for those who yearn for it. A friend of mine, an ordained minister, once said that he looked at faith the way a poor child looked at a fine gift in a brightly lit store window at Christmas time, wanting it but knowing that he would never be able to have it. If we are fortunate, our children may be able to have the gift of an untroubled faith, one that can give light to the world they live in, a gift of confidence and hope. That would be a fine gift indeed, but faith is not something anyone can demand in order to be a member of a community. Acceptance of ethical values, in contrast, *can* be a prerequisite of membership.

But still, isn't it somehow fraudulent to use the ethical system of a religion without the faith that gave it life in the first place? Again, many would say yes. But could it also be said that we are the psychologically injured victims of a period of cultural loss, and that we have no choice but to take such a less than ideal step in order to move forward again? Historically it has been in times of decline that the resurgence of religion has occurred, times when people's confidence in their powers and their ability to control events have been shaken. Rather than God-like, people come to see themselves as confused and in need of help. If religion is a crutch, it is at least one that enables people to walk better and to move ahead, even if haltingly, rather than continuing to stumble and fall. To argue whether religion is a crutch and a fiction or a reflection of man's higher instincts is almost beside the point. *The immediate question is whether it allows people to be better or not.*

Yet there is still the feeling among many people that religion is either unnecessary or inadequate to our present needs, and that we will be able to make our lives rich and full without it. We are so taken up with the spirit of the times that we still want to believe that coercion is not only unnecessary but wrong, and that it will only be through the full expression of every person's true humanity and creativity that the modern era will reach its fulfillment. *But to accept this today requires a greater leap of faith than religion ever required.*

We may ask, for example, where is the evidence to support the confident assertion that people acting purely in their own self-interest will produce anything but the hostilities and manipulations that characterize so much of our public life today? And if it were agreed that a new ethic was needed, where is the evidence that we could construct one that had even a fraction of the power and wisdom of ones that have stood the test of time? And would the process of trying to construct such a new system lead to anything more than interminable squabbling and splitting into factions? And would an ethical system based on reason and science achieve the transcendental meaning of the world's religions, which have been able to infuse life with meaning and hope through the ages?

It is in this process of asking ourselves what we could do compared to what our ancestors did that the true magnitude of their gifts to us becomes apparent. For example, what holidays have we been able to create that have a fraction of the emotional appeal or beauty of Christmas? Even today, when we have rejected a good part of our traditional heritage, imagine how different our lives would be without that which still remains, the multitude of kindnesses and charitable acts, to friends and strangers alike, that make life worthwhile. What if we all decided we were liberated from these too, or, as many people have decided, from being responsible for their children, from wasting time on volunteer activities, or from doing anything for their community that does not benefit them? How much colder our lives would be, and how much more government would have to provide (and how much less satisfactorily it would do it).

Rather than preserving this heritage, we, driven by our obsessions, have too often sought to further discredit it, saying that "guilt" or the "dead hand of the past" is what keeps us from doing the wonderful things we would otherwise be capable of doing if only we were truly free. We say that religion is part of the "system" that is holding us down or working against us. In fact, each of us is almost totally dependent on the "system" of culture; it is our way of life. If it broke down and was replaced by chaos, we would realize how dependent we are on it for our ongoing existence, and how helpless we would be without it.

Even if it is imperfect, this heritage is what we have to work with, the place we must start. The need is to revitalize it—to give it new life in the conditions we find ourselves in—and to do this it requires that we have a realistic idea of who we are. It means that, rather than seeing ourselves as God-like, we see that we are actually very ordinary human beings, subject to all the foibles human beings have always been capable of, and that it was only our powerful technology that made us think we were exceptional. When we accept a more humble view of ourselves, religion will once again have something to say to us, and we will resume the age-old quest to find meaning in our lives and harmony in our communities.

11
For Everything a Season

April is the cruellest month.
T. S. ELIOT, *The Wasteland*

When in April the sweet showers fall
And pierce the drought of March to the root, and all
The veins are bathed in liquor of such power
As brings about the engendering of the flowers . . .
Then people long to go on pilgrimages.
CHAUCER, *The Canterbury Tales*

We have had our season of abundance, have feasted on a bountiful harvest, and all things considered, it was an extraordinary experience. But if we fail to see that the season is turning, and recklessly plant seeds only to see them killed by the cold blasts of the winter of industrial civilization, then spring will be the cruelest time, afflicted by privation and strife, rather than a time of new life and hope.

Autumn is a different season, and even though it may not appeal to the youthful exuberance of this nation, it has its own pleasures. It is a quieter time, a time for reflection, to think about seasons past and those to come. It has its own significance too, its own source of hope, one that has long been valued in the East but is foreign to our expectation that progress is bound permanently into the American way. The *Tao-Te-Ching* is probably the fullest expression of this way of seeing life:

> *All things in nature work silently. They come into being and possess nothing. They fulfill their function and make no claim. All things alike do their work, and then we see them subside. When they have reached their bloom, each returns to its origins. Returning to their origin means rest, or fulfillment of destiny. This reversion is an eternal law. To know that law is wisdom.*

Our time of abundance will not go on forever, but neither will winter. Perhaps the first stirrings of a new spring are already being felt, the first new life as the grip of industrial society begins to weaken. If we can see it with the eyes of Chaucer's pilgrims, almost as children exploring the world for the first time and open to all its newness, it can be a good time, perhaps not great in the heroic sense, but good in the sense that it will offer the chance to enjoy the experience of being helpful without being taken advantage of, of being generous without feeling like a fool, and of knowing the security of shared loyalties and careful husbandry of the land and resources that the community relies on.

The force behind these explorations of the new season is cultural evolution, of people searching for what is fresh and vital, trying one thing and then perhaps another, but always moving away from that which is overripe and fading. It is a process of sensing the changes that are occurring in the world about us and of going with them rather than resisting them. In the process, we will learn what is lasting about our way of life and what is not, what will be held onto and what will be let go. What takes its place will reflect the more universal qualities of human existence, and even though the actual shapes and forms of the future cannot be foreseen, the central quest will be the same—what gives life meaning and satisfaction.

We cannot say very much about the process of cultural evolution or where it will take us; evolution is always an extremely complex process. Who would have predicted, looking at a lifeless planet in a lifeless solar system as the earth was 500 million years ago, the beginning of life and its elaboration, and the rapid evolution of human life? The complexity of evolution dwarfs the capacity of our computers, and especially of our computer programmers; it cannot be predicted. But knowing what we do about the *process* of evolution in the past and also the conditions under which it is occurring today, there is much that we can learn. We know with great certainty that humankind is now a major threat to the habitability of the earth household, and we must ask what it is from our past that we should guard against. Up to this point we have been talking about things that we should keep; it is also necessary to learn what to cast away.

We in the West have seen the process of evolution as an ascending process, with modern civilization at the apex, as opposed to the cyclical view of history in the East. Both have some truth. Over the eons evolution has led to the great proliferation of species and the increased richness of life on earth, to the slow filling of ecological niches. But this general trend has been made up of all manner of cyclical explosions of life and death; the dinosaurs are the rule rather than the exception. A temporary winner, in fact, is in the greatest danger because in their abundance they tend to overuse the environment they depend on, change it, and reduce its capacity to provide for their own needs. We are more at risk than the dinosaurs because we have greater capacity to change the environment than they did, and if we last the hundred million years the dinosaurs did, we will be lucky indeed. The lowly porcupine and other "primitive" species have survived the longest, and will undoubtedly outlast us unless we can achieve some sort of an ongoing balance with the environment that sustains us.

The measure of evolutionary success is survival, but we may be forgiven our anthropocentricity if we add another measure—the quality of life. The human mind has grown beyond its instincts, for good or ill, and is not satisfied with survival alone. Unlike the porcupine, we go to war or commit suicide if our minds are tormented enough, even if our physical needs are satisfied. We are looking for an evolutionary niche, but one which recognizes our human natures. It is not an easy task, especially given the point we have reached today, with an exploding world population making increasing demands on the land and its resources.

Looking at our evolutionary prospects, there would seem to be three things that we should consciously strive for, things that have not been characteristic of our past: tolerance, balance, and diversity.

Tolerance

Tolerance is one of those words that has almost become a platitude; everyone is for it, yet we still find all sorts of reasons to be outraged by what others do or say. We are a proud people, and we like it that way. The dark side of pride, however, is intolerance; our pride causes us to feel we must be right and others wrong, in everything—religion, politics, morals, on and on—and this as much as anything else has led to the violence which has characterized Western civilization.

The East has much to teach us here. In the Eastern religions, God is seen as a life force, the spiritual essence that is in all living things, as opposed to a God of a chosen people, favored over others. The Eastern belief leads directly toward tolerance and nonviolence; it is wrong even to kill animals since all living things have divinity within them. And rather than having to postulate a devil to explain evil (and to see the devil in all that oppose good), the East sees evil as the burying of one's divinity under selfish desires; the goal is to remove these encrustations of the spirit, to release one's divinity into the world, to express it in relationships with those around us, and ultimately to be united with the life force of the world. Hindus see all religions as different routes to this same end; all are equally valid. Gandhi adopted much of Christ's teachings with no difficulty whatsoever at a time of intense struggle with Christian England. It added to his spiritual beliefs, rather than warring with them as would be the case with us. Our prospects for evolutional success would be much better if we could follow Gandhi's lead.

There are different levels of tolerance. Between communities it is essential to let a thousand blossoms bloom, hoping as many as possible will thrive, yet knowing many will fail. In the evolutionary process, we learn as much from failures as from successes. Yet a community itself has to work if it is to survive; it will collapse if everyone goes in their own direction, as we learned from the American experiences with community. Yet a community becomes intolerable if there is no acceptance of the natural diversity among human beings and sees the true as simply a matter of saying yea or nay. Oppressive moral demands drive people away from community more surely than anything else.

Again, the East gives us an example of the more advanced position here. In India, there are four paths to God: pleasure, worldly success, duty, and release. Most people are at the first two stages, which is simply human nature. Hinduism makes no prohibitions on them, but only suggests that they will grow unsatisfying, and that individuals will come to the point of wanting to move on to the higher paths. Some individuals reach this point quickly and others never do, but each path is considered a part of life. How much more sensible this is than to harp on human weaknesses and to demand perfection, to, in effect, deny the different stages of individual development.

Balance

Balance has been a theme all through this book, but just asking for it is rarely enough. Balance is a subtle and often ambiguous position, one that is often quite out of keeping with this age of excess. The extremes, in contrast, are clear; ideological positions form around them, and debate attracts attention in a way that the quiet good sense of balance can never do. To go to the limits is challenging and exciting; we tend to honor those who try for the highest goals, even when they fail; to have tried and failed is better than to have never tried. We feel the need to stand away from the crowd and to criticize it as slavish and dull. If done frequently enough, as we do with the family for example, it causes the center to seem like a no-man's-land rather than the place where most people are, and indeed should be.

Imbalances, once they are established, are difficult to correct. The tendency is for change to swing like a pendulum from one extreme to the other. To escape from the excesses of individualism, people go toward drugs or alcohol or into cults where the leader's orders are accepted without question. To get away from an excess of untempered reason, people join religions that reject reason altogether. People react against huge cities by buying land as far away from anybody else as possible. We overreact to inflation and cause unemployment instead. Or one extreme generates the opposite one, as when political extremists of the left stimulate the right to counter it, or vice versa. Hopefully we will have the wisdom to see that one excess is no better than another; history is full of examples of peoples trapped by their hatreds —Ireland, Iran, Palestine, and even Russia, obsessed by the humiliations of foreign invaders.

But even when there are no hatreds and emotions, balance can still be difficult to find. It requires a sensitivity to many factors and may require long experience to find. The quest for an optimum size for human settlements offers an interesting example of the problems involved. Parallel studies done in small towns and big cities at first seem to confirm the popular stereotype, that people in small towns are different —friendlier and more helpful. Researchers who knocked on doors asking to use the phone to call about a broken-down car or who laid down on the sidewalk feigning sickness or drunkenness were more likely to be helped in small towns than in big cities, and more civilities were exchanged. But the matter is not quite that simple because people in small towns were also nosier and more apt to gossip about each other. The interpretation of these findings is that in cities the problem is *overload*—there are too many people to deal with —and therefore contacts must be avoided, ignored, cut short, or responded to coldly. Overload is the same thing that forces workers in mental institutions to adopt a cold professionalism in order to cope with so many disturbed people. In small towns, in contrast, the problem is *starvation*—there is not enough to occupy people—so they are curious to find out who the drunk on the sidewalk is so they can talk about him later on. It is not so much that people in cities and small towns are different as it is that they are in different situations. Balance, in this case, is not only having the *right amount* of human contact, it must be meaningful contact, not just passing people on a busy street or gossiping to pass the time. This will be easier in both city neighborhoods and small towns when social and economic activities are once again focused in smaller areas, bringing people into regular contact in the course of a day's activities.

A similar issue is the role of mobility in human society, but here balance is harder yet to achieve because, at best, something of value must be given up. High mobility tends to cause people to be more flexible, creative, and less narrow-minded, all desirable qualities, but it also increases mental strain, superficiality, cynicism, and reduces sensitivity and responsibility, rather like a satiated tourist with little interest or concern for the countries going by outside the train window. Low mobility, on the other hand, tends to lead to just the opposite qualities, to narrow-mindedness and inflexibility, but with less mental strain and cynicism, and a much deeper knowledge and understanding of the smaller world lived in. The modern temperament tends to assume that it is possible to have the good qualities of both high and low mobility without the bad, and this causes us to be dissatisfied with a situation that may in fact be well balanced between being a perennial tourist and having one's life bounded by a village.

Even philosophers have delighted in arguing the extremes. The question of whether man is basically good or bad, a central theme in Western thought, disregards the vast evidence that every person has within them the potential for both. The old question of determinism versus free will—whether it is culture and history that shapes people's actions or whether individuals act on their own free will—ignores the interplay of both factors in all human affairs. We distinguish rigidly between fact and value when it is our values that determine the facts we are interested in. Nature and nurture—genes and environment—both shape the development of a child. We even make a rigid separation between man and nature rather than seeing man as a part of nature, which we assuredly are.

Many of the imbalances in our society will tend to correct themselves as affluence passes, but some will get worse, and these are the ones that people, not surprisingly, fear the most. The economy will require a great deal of restraint and patience if we are to avoid the twin pitfalls of runaway inflation and depression. And the frustrations generated in the process could cause the political pendulum to swing widely between left and right, adding the fear of political deterioration to the fear of economic breakdown. But if resource scarcity cannot keep us from our excesses, it can at least reduce the power with which we can pursue them. We will have less wealth to build military weapons, to prop up corrupt foreign governments, or to build grandiose construction projects. And when we are less able to influence other nations, we will be more apt to accept them for what they are—independent nations trying to make their own way as best they can. In the same way, we will have to accept more diversity in this country, and not assume, as we so often do, that people living in different ways are criticizing our ways. Diversity, in fact, rather than being a threat to our internal stability, is one of the strongest forces working in our favor by encouraging cultural evolution.

Diversity

It is possible that the reader may have the impression from reading this far that restraints on individualism may reduce the diversity in our society today. We think of our society as incredibly diverse, and in a superficial sense, I suppose this is true—all the new products, fashions, the "new waves" of this and that. But this masks a great *absence* of diversity in the way we support ourselves. We must not confuse the *complexity* of our economy with the fact that all of us are now dependent on the smooth function of *one system*, the worldwide industrial economy. This is just the opposite of diversity.

It is rare that a single quality is valuable in all circumstances; even the best of things usually have some disadvantages. But with diversity, the disadvantages are hard to find, while the benefits seem to be universal. Diversity in itself is an attractive quality, avoiding the monotony of cities that all look the same, agricultural regions where only one crop is grown, or societies where people all seem to be the same, as in totalitarian countries. But diversity has a much more fundamental advantage for survival: *It contributes to stability, to the ongoing continuity of life and the avoidance of devastating breakdowns.* Diversity means that no part of a system is so dominant that its collapse would be a catastrophe for all. With diversity, if one element broke, others would be there to take over and keep the whole from collapsing. Diversity also allows change to occur smoothly since individuals can shift to modestly different ways without making big, risky changes, to experiment with greater safety, and thus encourage it. The diversity in human beings is perhaps the most valuable diversity of all; imagine the instability there would be in our economy if all Americans responded to the same economic conditions in the same way, all deciding to buy or sell stocks at the same time, take their money out of the bank, or buy land in the country? Or imagine the terror that would be loose in the world today if human nature were easier to meld into the plans of totalitarian rulers?

But working against the myriad natural tendencies toward diversity is the industrial economy, which for so long has pulled everything into its grip, not only in this country but worldwide. Now every country has to worry about a recession that originates in the United States, a cutoff in Mideastern oil supplies, or a financial crisis in Latin America. But the trends that are so ominous for industrial society also suggest a return to diversity. Financial stringencies are already forcing less developed countries to shift their attention from trade to making do with their own resources. In this country, slowdown is threatening a number of our largest industries, which only a few years ago seemed invulnerable; if they go under, many openings for smaller, more decentralized businesses will be created immediately to fill the void left. Cities which are dependent on one industry are going through the wringer, but depressed rents for housing and commercial spaces will encourage businesses to move in that were not profitable at the higher prices prior to the downturn. Regions with a great deal of natural diversity—the ones the large farm machines did not fit into—are attracting people with their diverse resources—soils, timber, building materials, and water supplies. The use of local resources will help reestablish the regional diversity that once characterized this country, diversity of buildings, foods, and jobs. With less interstate trade, the power of the federal government to regulate virtually everything will be reduced, and with reduced dependency on foreign trade, it will become more difficult to mobilize support for military activities in distant countries. Just as energy abundance produced the powerful movement toward centralization, the shift toward land and renewable resources will, just as inevitably, lead toward the smaller, more flexible ways of diversity.

The fear of breakdown in the world industrial economy is a real one, but in other cases the fear of the loss of a centralized system is exaggerated. The social security system provides a good example. If it broke down, a great deal of hardship and poverty would undoubtedly be caused (and I am certainly not recommending it), but we should not make the problems created larger than life either. It would mean, for the most part, a return to the older supports of family, supplemented by community and religious groups. These institutions are weak now (partly because their traditional functions were taken up by government), but they would automatically be strengthened if social security broke down. It would encourage parents, for example, to raise their children with care because they may be dependent on them in their old age. Individuals would not be so apt to flaunt community values if they may need the community's help some day. And the same is true of helping others; in a sense it is an investment in the future, because no one knows when they may need help themselves.

We hear about the advantages of diversity when it fits into the dominant trends in our society, such as the economic diversity of cities, but little about it in all the other cases where current trends work against diversity. The extended family is only one of many possible examples. When the breadwinner of a nuclear family is laid off, a desperate situation can develop if unemployment benefits run out and another job is not found. In an extended family, in contrast, the loss of one job means that the overall family income has been reduced much more modestly, and the wider array of contacts, skills, and resources of the extended family can help get by even if another job is not found.

The question of which types of energy we should develop, whether we should follow a "hard" energy path of nuclear energy, coal, or synthetic fuels, or a "soft" energy path of renewable resources and conservation, is easily answered; we should follow all of them, but each on a modest scale and only until we see where they lead. In rough outline, this is what we have done, except in a few instances, most notably nuclear energy, which had such powerful industrial and bureaucratic support. But even though this led to the waste of a great deal of money, we at least know that nuclear energy is not the panacea it was projected to be. Without spending the money, there would still be a chorus of voices saying that nuclear energy is our salvation, and people, being only human, would want to believe this to be true. Leaving any path unexplored is to take a risk, the kind of risk that diversity protects against.

The advantages of diversity are clearest in the natural world. Complex natural environments, such as tropical rain forests and temperate grasslands, do not suffer the outbursts of life and death common to simpler environments such as islands that are isolated from continental evolution and arctic environments that are kept simple by harsh conditions. In diverse environments, competition among many species does not allow any single species to build up its numbers to dangerous levels. Overpopulation radically constricts the alternatives available to any species to provide for its ongoing needs, threatening it with environmental degradation and then population decline.

Our industrial agriculture is very productive, but this is achieved by increased scale and specialization. Losses from insects are greater today than when DDT was first introduced in the early forties. Part of this is due to the fact that insects have developed resistance to insecticides, but part of it is due to the reduced diversity of American agriculture. Monoculture is often necessary for a farmer to make a living, but it increases his economic risks as well as the ecological risks. He can be bankrupted by low prices for his crop as easily as he can by bad weather or plant diseases. In a traditional society, the farmer's situation is completely different. He plants a number of crops in order to use his labor fully all season long, but this also provides protection against unusual weather conditions—hot or cold, wet or dry—since some of what he plants is bound to produce well even if several of his crops are wiped out. And with many different crops to sell, something will fetch a good price in the market so that he can buy the things he and his family need.

The Pleasures of the New Season

To fear change is a very human thing. Change threatens that which we value, with no assurance that anything of value will take its place. But in fact there are assurances, of a sort anyway: things that are lost do not just disappear into a void; something takes their place. And it is not only the good things that will be lost; unpleasant things too will go. If the ease and wealth of industrial society are reduced, so would be the traffic, the pollution, the toxic wastes, and the noise. Reduced mobility would mean a more constricted world, but we would know the smaller world we lived in intimately, both the natural and the social components. Less use of fossil fuels would mean more physical work but would leave us with cleaner air, making us healthier and more in control of our own needs. Working with others can be frustrating, but it can be satisfying as well.

It was the less affluent and less mobile world of the past that permitted the enjoyment of simple pleasures, the ones which today are no match for the garish ones advertised so insistently. We have grown insensitive to the subtle pleasures of the senses, of being able to enjoy the beauty of a single flower or a piece of fruit, the smell of a summer shower, the sounds of leaves rustling in a breeze or children laughing. Such things were deemed to have little value in an age of excess. The same is true of the pleasures that have their origins in our instincts. What enjoyments does the consumer society have to offer that are as satisfying as taking a bath when tired and dirty, sitting down to a good meal when hungry, falling into a bed after a hard day's work, being warmed when cold, or taking a long drink out of a clear stream while on a long hike? In a sense, these instinctive pleasures do more than simply feel good; they feel right—there is no question of whether they are the correct thing to do or not. None have to be learned, and they are available to everyone. But this was their problem in our society; they were not exclusive—no one could be excluded from enjoying them—and so our society accorded them no status, and they have been all but forgotten. And then we go to the other extreme with sex, the one instinct that cultures have universally restrained, and build it up out of all proportion simply because it is not indiscriminately available like the other instinctive pleasures, and therefore offers the chance to perform, to excel.

But these are the simple pleasures. What about the spectacular ones, the supreme experiences of life whatever the words used to describe them—joy, ecstasy, peak experience, fulfillment, or simply happiness? This is of course an intensely personal matter as well as a very complex one, but still it is surprising that it is completely avoided in the scientific literature. The annual compendium of psychological publications, *Psychological Abstracts*, runs to over a thousand pages of double-columned entries, but includes only the word *happiness* among its multitudinous subject headings, and the entries under it comprise roughly an *eighth* of a page, less than the heading of handwriting that precedes it. And the articles listed deal primarily with satisfaction—with jobs, living conditions, and spouses—rather than happiness. The scientific method evidently cannot deal with this most important of matters.

In the rush of our lives, we often fail to think about such things, but it is important to stop for a moment and consider what have been the best moments in our lives, the ones to be savored time and time again. Poets and others who are willing to bare their souls on these matters usually speak of them as experiences of unity or oneness—with nature, with another person when in love, or with the spiritual unity of all life in a religious experience. Even scientists, when making a great discovery, speak of the experience as everything falling into place, again, of unity. Perhaps this simply reflects the orientation of those who put their feelings onto paper, but still it is striking how rarely there are statements of individual achievement or winning over competitors. Is this because we are modest? It hardly seems likely in this age when anything can be said. The more likely explanation is that winning separates the winner from the others, breaks the unity that is the source of satisfaction. Perhaps the spirit of this age, dominated as it is by individual success, only served to work against the things that make us feel good, creating isolation and a bewildered kind of suffering instead of happiness.

One of the handful of studies dealing with happiness was done by Bernard Rimland and described in *Psychological Reports* (1982, Vol. 51). He first asked college students to list the people they knew best, then asked them to note whether they were happy or unhappy, and then after this was done, to note whether each were selfish or not, selfishness being defined as a stable tendency to devote their time to their own interests and, in so doing, to be too busy to help others. Only 78 selfish people were reported to be happy, compared to 827 unselfish people. Rimland comments:

> *The findings represent an interesting paradox: Selfish people are, by definition, those whose activities are devoted to bringing themselves happiness. Yet, at least as judged by others, these selfish people are far less likely to be happy than those whose efforts are devoted to making others happy.*

Why selflessness and feelings of oneness and unity should be so satisfying after centuries of conditioning in just the opposite direction is an interesting question. We all know how good it feels to help other people, even those whom we will never see again. It almost has the quality of an instinct about it, of feeling right. Could this be the result of the long era of human evolution in which hunters and gatherers had to share in order to survive? Certainly this obligation to share is universally reported in the earliest contacts with primitive people as well as in the remaining hunting and gathering tribes that still survive. Those groups or individuals that did not share did not survive, extinguishing the "selfish genes." We were left with the "sharing genes," the ones we are frustrating in our individualistic, acquisitive way of life. These could very well provide us with the greatest pleasures of the new season, of helping others and being helped in return.

The New Wealth

Even with all the wealth generated during the last decades, Americans rarely saw themselves as wealthy. There was always someone else who had things we did not have, things that made them clearly "rich," but not us. In fact we are all wealthy, or most of us anyway. Think of what we have compared to those who are blind, in wheelchairs, mentally retarded, or emotionally disturbed by childhood experiences. To think so much about what we do not have rather than what we are blessed with can perhaps be blamed on the needs of the economy, but even so, it is not flattering to us as a nation. It is almost as if we are a nation of spoiled children, having indulged ourselves but still feeling we need more to be happy. Rather than yearning for what cannot be, we should realize that we have a great deal, all of us, and the key is to use well what we have.

We have much, but a good deal of our wealth today is based on the oil and gas still left in the ground; it is what makes our machines useful. As these premium fuels are depleted, much of what we have built for ourselves will lose value, and that is bound to hurt people. The time to build anew is now, while energy is still available to build with, but this is difficult; it is such an ambiguous time. It is hard to build around renewable resources, for example, when there is still oil in the ground and the industrial economy still has power left in it. And the machines are alluring; just as with television, it is so easy to sit back and let them work for us; they demand so little, physically, intellectually, and emotionally. Or at least so it seems, until we remember that we are dependent on the machines and have organized our lives around them so they can work as efficiently as possible, regardless of the impact on people.

But hard realities are already cutting into the world we know, and because of this, there are bridges being built between the old ways and the new. In order to find a job, it is increasingly necessary to make it oneself, to be self-employed. In order to build, it is increasingly necessary to build on a smaller scale with simpler tools and materials, often by hand, but building in a way that is both cheaper and more permanent. It is to build with the help of friends, rather than through loan officers, contractors, labor unions, and bureaucrats. It means to work hard, yes, and to see things go slowly, but to be free of heavy debts and worries about how they will be paid. And it means to have the confidence of knowing that the work will have value no matter what happens in the mainstream economy. One of the strongest reasons for wanting to distance ourselves from the industrial economy is to be less concerned with a national debt grown to unmanageable size, government policies that can make or break one's job or business, or an oil embargo that could ruin one's hopes for the future.

But the most important reason to distance oneself from the industrial economy is simply because it means a better life, less affluent, true, but richer in other ways, richer in the more important ways. It means to avoid the poverty of the spirit that comes from seeing wealth only in terms of what we can accumulate, and seeing it as well in the ongoing life of a family and the collective wealth of a community. It means to gain respect in proportion to what is done to enrich a community, rather than what is taken from it in private gain. It means to establish a way of life that encourages people's best instincts, rather than frustrates them. It means to work with nature rather than against it, to make the land that sustains a community fruitful and productive as well as beautiful. It means to have work be "as love made visible," love for those around us and for the land that sustains a way of life.

There is a time for everything, and wisdom is to know what is appropriate for our times, what to take forward and what to leave behind. A good part of this simply means to take things as they come, enjoying what the times have to offer us, many of which are universal to all human life. We have had our time of affluence, and now the individuals who are fortunate are those who will not miss it, those who realize that it is in thinking of something larger than ourselves that we enrich our own lives. These are the people who, rather than fearing the future, can look forward to it with confidence and hope.

Acknowledgments

The university libraries were surprisingly unhelpful in this project. Beyond some anthropologists and historians, who deal with different cultures and different times, there were few who spoke of traditional ways in a positive voice. To do so would be to open a writer to the charge of romanticism, as if modern ways were somehow universal while the ways of the past are only a historical aberration. For the most part, traditions are generally depicted as holdovers from the past and often stand in the way of progress and economic development.

The libraries were most disappointing in the field of religion. Other disciplines, even the humanities and liberal arts, can employ an analytic, scientific approach with some success—the only one that is academically respectable—but this method misses the essence of religion. For this reason, I am particularly indebted to George N. Monsma of Calvin College for his paper "Biblical Principles and Economic Theory," on which a good deal of the section on biblical economics rests. I would not have known how much contradiction there was between our economic system and our religious heritage without it.

My main debts, however, lie with the people, both in this country and around the world, whose actions are the best source of information on older ways. I have been fortunate in being able to travel over the years, in Europe, Asia, and Africa, and everywhere there are things to be learned. India especially was full of surprises. I expected to find decay and deterioration—which there is—but I found amazing sophistication and richness as well. Having a research grant to study the energy used in Amish agriculture forced me to approach them, and once their reserve toward outsiders was passed, speaking with the Amish people was a wonderful experience. It is to these peoples, who held on to their ways in the face of all the modern pressures, that I wish to acknowledge my debts. I can only hope that I have not done too much injustice to them.

More specifically, I owe much to my wife, Martha, who is my best editor and critic. A valued adviser and friend is Gary Suttle, a former student who, because of his gentleness and graciousness, does not fit well into this ungentle and ungracious world. I especially wish to thank Joseph Spieler for his support and encouragement when others shied away from a project that spoke positively of traditional ways. Jerry Gross not only contributed his good editorial skills to the project but was a pleasure to work with as well. Tucker Childs and Mr. and Mrs. Leonard Shurtleff provided generous help in the final stages of manuscript preparation. A major influence on this book has been my two sons, Aaron and Blake, who, while not taking part in it directly, have shaped its hopes and aspirations.

Bibliography

Chapter 1

Adams, Henry. *The Degradation of the Democratic Dogma.* New York: Macmillan, 1919.

Brown, Lester. *Building a Sustainable Society.* New York: Norton, 1981.

Ellul, Jacques. *The Technological Society.* New York: Random House/Vintage Books, 1964.

Hawken, Paul. *The Next Economy.* New York: McGraw-Hill, 1983.

Heilbroner, Robert L. *An Inquiry into the Human Prospect.* New York: Norton, 1974.

Hofstadter, Richard. *Social Darwinism in American Thought.* Boston: Beacon, 1955.

Johnson, Warren. *Muddling Toward Frugality.* Boulder: Shambhala Publications, 1979.

Kahn, Herman. *The Coming Boom.* New York: Simon and Schuster, 1982.

Kropotkin, Peter. *Mutual Aid.* Boston: Extending Horizons Books, 1902.

Lasch, Christopher. *The Culture of Narcissism.* New York: Warner Books, 1979.

Naisbitt, John. *Megatrends: Ten New Directions Transforming Our Lives.* New York: Warner Books, 1982.

Rifkin, Jeremy, with Ted Howard. *Entropy: A New World View.* New York: Viking Press, 1980.

Sahlins, Marshall D. "The Origins of Society." *Scientific American.* September 1960, pp. 76–87.

Schumacher, E. F. *Small Is Beautiful.* New York: Perennial, 1973.

Slater, Philip. *The Pursuit of Loneliness: American Culture at the Breaking Point.* Boston: Beacon, 1976.

Snyder, Gary. *Earth House Hold.* New York: New Directions, 1969.

———. *The Old Way: Six Essays.* San Francisco: City Lights, 1977.

Stavrianos, L. C. *The Promise of the Coming Dark Ages.* San Francisco: W. H. Freeman, 1976.

Chapter 2

Berry, Wendell. *The Unsettling of America.* San Francisco: Sierra Club Press, 1978.

Boulding, Kenneth. *The Meaning of the Twentieth Century.* New York: Harper & Row, 1965.

Daly, Herman E. *Steady State Economics.* San Francisco: Freeman, 1977.

Elgin, Duane. *Voluntary Simplicity: Toward A Way of Life that is Outwardly Simple, Inwardly Rich.* New York: Morrow, 1981.

Ferkiss, Victor. *The Future of Technological Civilization.* New York: Braziller, 1974.

Georgescu-Roegen, Nicholas. *Energy and Economic Myths.* Elmsford, N.Y.: Pergamon Press, 1977.

———. *The Entropy Law and the Economic Process.* Cambridge, Mass.: Harvard University Press, 1971.

Heilbroner, Robert L. *Business Civilization in Decline.* New York: Norton, 1976.

Hirsch, Fred. *Social Limits to Growth.* Cambridge, Mass.: Harvard University Press, 1978.

Ophuls, William. *Ecology and the Politics of Scarcity.* San Francisco: Freeman, 1977.

Chapter 3

Lovins, Amory. *Soft Energy Paths.* New York: Ballinger, 1977.

Snyder, Gary. *The Real Work.* New York: New Directions, 1980.

World Coal Study. *Coal: A Bridge to the Future.* New York: Harper and Row, 1982.

Chapter 4

Eckholm, Erick and Frank Record. "The Affluent Diet: A Worldwide Health Hazard." *The Futurist,* February 1977, p. 18.

Illich, Ivan. *Medical Nemesis: The Expropriation of Health.* New York: Bantam, 1977.

Kern, Ken. *The Owner Built House.* New York: Scribners, 1975.

Kunz, Jeffrey R. M., ed. American Medical Association, *Family Medical Guide.* New York: Random House, 1982.

Lappe, Francis Moore. *Diet for a Small Planet.* New York: Ballantine, 1975.

Mazira, Edward. *Passive Solar Energy Book.* Emmaus, Pa.: Rodale Press, 1979.

Rapoport, Amos. *House Form and Culture.* Englewood Cliffs, N.J.: Prentice-Hall, 1969.

Stoner, Carol H. *Producing Your Own Power.* Emmaus, Pa.: Rodale Press, 1974.

Chapter 5

Durant, Will. *Our Oriental Heritage.* New York: Simon and Schuster, 1935.

Hardin, Garrett. "The Tragedy of the Commons." *Science,* December 13, 1968, pp. 1243–1248.

Polanyi, Karl. *The Great Transformation.* Boston: Beacon Press, 1944.

Potter, David M. *People of Plenty: Economic Abundance and the American Character.* Chicago: University of Chicago Press, 1954.

Chapter 6

Illich, Ivan. *Gender.* New York: Pantheon, 1982.

Mitchell, G. *Human Sex Differences: A Primatologist's Perspective.* New York: Van Nostrand Reinhold, 1981.

Chapter 7

Berry, Wendell. *The Country of Marriage.* New York: Harcourt Brace Jovanovich, 1975.

Burns, Scott. *Home, Inc: The Hidden Wealth and Power of the American Household.* New York: Doubleday, 1975.

Lasch, Christopher. *Haven in a Heartless World: The Family Beseiged.* New York: Basic Books, 1979.

Laslett, Peter, ed. *Household and Family in Past Times.* New York: Cambridge University Press, 1972.

———. *The World We Have Lost: England Before the Industrial Age.* New York: Scribners, 1971.

Pearce, Joseph C. *Magical Child.* New York: Dutton, 1977.

Chapter 8

Bailey, F. G. "The Peasant View of the Bad Life," *British Association for the Advancement of Science,* December 1966, pp. 400–401.

Berry, Wendell. *The Gift of Good Land and Further Essays Cultural and Agricultural.* Berkeley: North Point Press, 1981.

Forrester, Jay. *Collected Papers of Jay W. Forrester.* Cambridge: MIT Press, 1975.

Hostetler, John A. *Amish Society.* Baltimore: Johns Hopkins Press, 1974.

Illich, Ivan. *Tools for Conviviality.* New York: Harper and Row, 1980.

Johnson, Warren. "Energy Conservation in Amish Agriculture." *Science*, Oct. 28, 1977, pp. 373–78.

Nisbet, Robert A. *The Quest For Community*. New York: Oxford University Press, 1962.

Zablozki, Benjamin. *The Joyful Community*. New York: Penguin, 1972.

Chapter 9

Alexander, Christopher. *The Pattern Language*. New York: Oxford University Press, 1977.

———. *The Timeless Way of Building*. New York: Oxford University Press, 1979.

Jacobs, Jane. *The Death and Life of Great American Cities*. New York: Vintage Books, 1961.

King, F. H. *Farmers of Forty Centuries*. New York: Harcourt, Brace & Co., 1911.

McHarg, Ian. *Design With Nature*. New York: Doubleday, 1969.

———. *Architecture Without Architects*. New York: Doubleday, 1969.

Rudofsky, Bernard. *Streets for People: A Primer for Americans*. New York: Van Nostrand Reinhold, 1982.

Chapter 10

Bellah, Robert N. *The Broken Covenant*. New York: Seabury Press, 1975.

Durant, Will. *The Age of Faith*. New York: Simon and Schuster, 1950.

Fromm, Eric. *Escape From Freedom*. New York: Holt, Rinehart and Winston, 1963.

Iyer, Raghavan. *The Moral and Political Thought of Mahatma Gandhi*. New York: Oxford University Press, 1973.

Jung, C. G. *Psychological Reflections: A New Anthology of His Writings, 1905–1961*. Princeton: Princeton University Press, 1970.

Lings, Martin. *Ancient Beliefs and Modern Superstitions.* London: Perennial Books, 1964.

Simpson, George G. "The Search for an Ethic." In *The Meaning of Evolution.* New Haven: Yale University Press, 1949.

Tawney, R. H. *Religion and the Rise of Capitalism.* New York: Harcourt, Brace, 1926.

Weber, Max. *The Protestant Ethic and the Spirit of Capitalism.* New York: Scribners, 1958.

Chapter 11

Dubos, Rene. *Celebrations of Life.* New York: McGraw-Hill, 1981.

———. *Of Human Diversity.* Worcester, Massachusetts: Clark University Press, 1974.

———. *The Resiliance of Ecosystems.* Boulder: Colorado Associated University Presses, 1978.

Jeffers, Robinson. *Not Man Apart.* David Brower, ed. San Francisco: Sierra Club Press, 1965.

Kuhn, Thomas S. *The Structure of Scientific Revolutions.* Chicago: University of Chicago Press, 1970.

Meeker, Joseph W. *The Comedy of Survival: Studies in Literary Ecology.* New York: Scribners, 1974.

Piper, Joseph. *Fortitude and Temperance.* London: Faber and Faber, 1955.

———. *Justice.* London: Faber and Faber, 1957.

———. *Prudence.* London: Faber and Faber, 1960.

Toffler, Alvin. *Future Shock.* New York: Random House, 1970.

Index